· Southern Living ·
Rotisserie
Chicken Cookbook

Easy Chicken and
Dumplings, page 59

·Southern Living·
Rotisserie
Chicken Cookbook

101 Hearty Recipes with Store-Bought Convenience

Oxmoor
House®

Welcome

Pick up a rotisserie chicken and bring home a meal.
When you want the perfect shortcut to weeknight meals, school lunches, or weekend entertaining, look no further than the deli section of your local grocery. By adding a perfectly seasoned and roasted chicken to your favorite recipes, you are adding rich flavor with little effort. Your dishes will taste like they took all day to make, but you'll know that the time-saving secret is a rotisserie chicken.

We at *Southern Living* love food that's comforting and full of flavor, and we know that there are ways to get those dishes on the table in less time than you would think. On every page, you will find our favorite kitchen tips that go even beyond using a rotisserie chicken. From **"Simple Swap"** tips that offer easy ingredient substitutions to **"Grab and Go!"** suggestions for what to pick up to complete your meal, we're going to help you get a homemade meal on the table in no time.

With **70 of our favorite rotisserie chicken recipes** and more than 2 dozen recipes for sides, cooking comforting meals for your family and friends is now easier and faster than ever before. From salads, pizzas, and sandwiches to pastas, casseroles, and soups, *Southern Living Rotisserie Chicken Cookbook* is packed with every recipe you need to bring exciting new dishes to your dining table.

Southern Living.

Contents

Rotisserie Chicken: The Breakdown

A step-by-step guide to cutting up a whole rotisserie chicken

Getting Started

- It's easiest to cut up a rotisserie chicken when it's warm; either cut it up as soon as you come home from the store, or warm the chicken for 15 minutes in a 350° oven.
- Cut all twine from the chicken, including the pieces that tie the legs together.

- If at all possible, use a boning knife to break down the chicken. The thin, narrow blade makes it easy to cut into tight spaces accurately and cleanly.
- The average chicken yields about 3 cups chopped or shredded meat.

Next, Add the Chicken!

Preparing your chicken for each recipe

shredded: take 2 forks, and pull chicken in opposite directions to make shreds
- perfect for saucy dishes like pastas and casseroles
- great way to use every bit of rotisserie chicken

chopped: cut chicken breast into bite-size cubes
- helps the chicken hold its shape in the finished dish

sliced: slice chicken breast into ¼-inch slices
- makes a beautiful presentation when topping a dish with chicken

1. Start by removing the legs. Place the chicken on a cutting board, breast side up. Pull the leg and thigh away from the chicken, and cut through the connective joint.

2. To separate the thigh from the drumstick, pull the drumstick away from the thigh, and cut through the connective joint.

3. Make a deep horizontal cut above each wing.

4. Make a deep vertical cut along both sides of the breastbone.

5. Remove the breast meat to chop or shred, or carve it in slices, starting from the outer edges and working inward.

6. Remove the wings from the chicken by pulling the wing away from the chicken body, and cutting through the wing joint.

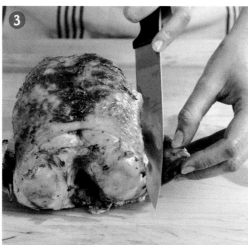

Take Stock of the Pantry

Save time and money by keeping a well-stocked pantry!

Oils, Vinegars, and Condiments

- ☐ balsamic vinegar
- ☐ barbecue sauce
- ☐ broth: beef, chicken, and vegetable
- ☐ Buffalo sauce
- ☐ canola or vegetable oil
- ☐ capers
- ☐ chili sauce
- ☐ cider vinegar
- ☐ cooking spray
- ☐ dressings: Ranch, blue cheese, honey-mustard
- ☐ ketchup
- ☐ mayonnaise
- ☐ mustard: yellow and Dijon
- ☐ olive oil
- ☐ peanut butter
- ☐ peanut oil
- ☐ pesto sauce
- ☐ red and white wine
- ☐ red and white wine vinegar
- ☐ sesame oil
- ☐ soy sauce
- ☐ Worcestershire sauce

Grains and Pasta

- ☐ all-purpose baking mix
- ☐ all-purpose flour
- ☐ baking powder
- ☐ baking soda
- ☐ cornmeal
- ☐ couscous
- ☐ dried breadcrumbs
- ☐ egg noodles
- ☐ fettuccine, rotini, and spaghetti
- ☐ panko breadcrumbs
- ☐ quick-cooking barley
- ☐ rice
- ☐ rice noodles
- ☐ self-rising cornmeal mix

Spice Rack

- ☐ bay leaves
- ☐ black peppercorns (grind fresh)
- ☐ chili powder
- ☐ curry powder
- ☐ dried basil
- ☐ dried dill
- ☐ dried oregano
- ☐ dried rosemary
- ☐ dried thyme
- ☐ dry mustard

- ☐ garlic powder
- ☐ ground cinnamon
- ☐ ground cumin
- ☐ ground ginger
- ☐ ground nutmeg
- ☐ paprika
- ☐ red pepper: crushed and ground
- ☐ salt
- ☐ sesame seeds
- ☐ taco seasoning

Canned Goods

- ☐ Alfredo sauce
- ☐ artichoke hearts
- ☐ beans: white, black, pinto
- ☐ black-eyed peas
- ☐ corn: cream-style and whole kernel
- ☐ cream of celery soup
- ☐ cream of chicken soup
- ☐ cream of mushroom soup
- ☐ diced pimientos
- ☐ diced tomatoes
- ☐ enchilada sauce
- ☐ green chiles
- ☐ pizza sauce
- ☐ roasted red peppers

Smart-Shopper Meals

Let the store do all the work with these "Grab and Go!" solutions. Start with a rotisserie chicken, add these recipe-free side dishes, and you've got a meal in a snap!

small carafe of dressing   deli salad (with toppings)

steamed green beans   bakery rolls (buttered)

deli potato salad

steamed broccoli/cauliflower

hummus and baby carrots

pita wedges

stir-fry vegetables

sliced almonds

cheesy rice and broccoli

deli garlic bread (toasted)

Bistro Grilled
Chicken Pizza

EVERYDAY EASY

simple main dishes for busy weeknights

Southwest Chicken Mac and Cheese

Makes 4 servings **Hands-on Time:** 20 min. **Total Time:** 20 min.

Homemade cheese sauce makes all the difference in this spicy twist on the classic standby.

½ (16-oz.) package rotini pasta
¼ cup butter
¼ cup all-purpose flour
2½ cups 2% reduced-fat milk
½ tsp. salt
¼ tsp. ground red pepper
⅛ tsp. garlic powder

1 (10-oz.) block 2% reduced-fat sharp Cheddar cheese, shredded
2 cups chopped rotisserie chicken
1 (10-oz.) can diced tomatoes and green chiles, drained
2 Tbsp. sliced green onions

1. Prepare pasta according to package directions.
2. Meanwhile, melt butter in a large saucepan over medium heat. Gradually whisk in flour until smooth; cook, whisking constantly, 1 minute. Gradually whisk in milk and next 3 ingredients; cook, whisking constantly, 8 to 10 minutes or until thickened. Remove from heat.
3. Gradually stir in Cheddar cheese, stirring until cheese is melted and sauce is smooth. Stir in chicken, tomatoes and green chiles, and hot cooked pasta. Sprinkle with green onions, and serve immediately.

FROM THE KITCHEN

Buying a block of cheese and shredding it at home is worth it. The cheese will melt faster, and your dinner will be ready even sooner.

Grab and Go!

To make this cheesy meal complete, pick up a bag of salad for a simple, healthy side dish.

❑ *1 bag of salad*

❑ *1 bottle of your favorite dressing*

If you love Fettuccine Alfredo but miss a little crunch, try this herb-flavored spin on a classic with crisp sugar snap peas.

Fettuccine with Chicken and Creamy Herb Sauce

Makes 2 servings **Hands-on Time:** 8 min. **Total Time:** 12 min.

6 oz. uncooked fettuccine
1¾ cups milk
1 (1-oz.) envelope garlic-herb soup mix
1 cup shredded rotisserie chicken
½ cup sugar snap peas
¼ cup (1 oz.) shredded Parmesan cheese
1 Tbsp. chopped fresh parsley
Freshly ground pepper

1. Cook fettuccine according to package directions.
2. Meanwhile, whisk together milk and soup mix in a 2-qt. saucepan; bring to a boil, stirring constantly. Add chicken and peas; reduce heat, and simmer 3 minutes or until chicken is well heated. Toss with fettuccine; sprinkle with Parmesan, parsley, and freshly ground pepper.

Simple Swap

If you don't have sugar snap peas on hand, you can substitute frozen broccoli. Just steam, and add in place of the peas.

FROM THE KITCHEN

By using garlic-herb soup mix, you are adding lots of flavor in just one step, saving you time and money.

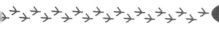
Chicken-Asparagus Mac and Cheese

Makes 4 servings **Hands-on Time:** 20 min. **Total Time:** 20 min.

½ (16-oz.) package rotini pasta
1 lb. fresh asparagus, cut into 1-inch pieces
¼ cup butter
¼ cup all-purpose flour
2½ cups 2% reduced-fat milk
½ tsp. salt
¼ tsp. ground red pepper
⅛ tsp. garlic powder
1 (10-oz.) block 2% reduced-fat sharp Cheddar cheese, shredded
2 cups chopped rotisserie chicken

1. Prepare pasta according to package directions. Add asparagus pieces to pasta during last 3 minutes of cooking. Drain and set aside.

2. Meanwhile, melt butter in a large saucepan over medium heat. Gradually whisk in flour until smooth; cook, whisking constantly, 1 minute. Gradually whisk in milk and next 3 ingredients; cook, whisking constantly, 8 to 10 minutes or until thickened. Remove from heat.

3. Gradually stir in Cheddar cheese, stirring until cheese is melted and sauce is smooth. Stir in chicken, hot cooked pasta, and asparagus. Serve immediately.

If this Mac and Cheese isn't cheesy enough for you, sprinkle a little more shredded Cheddar on top!

Simple Swap

You can substitute frozen asparagus in this recipe for fresh. Just add to pasta during the last minute of cooking.

Grab and Go!

Pair this entrée with sliced and toasted French bread for a complete meal that's ready in minutes.

❑ *1 loaf French bread*

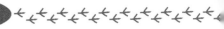

Wide egg noodles are just the right pasta to hold all that cream sauce— and they add rich flavor to this simple pasta dish.

FROM THE KITCHEN

To make this dish extra special, top with additional Parmesan cheese and chopped parsley.

Creamy Chicken and Noodles

Makes 6 servings **Hands-on Time:** 6 min. **Total Time:** 20 min.

1 (8-oz.) package wide egg noodles
2 Tbsp. butter, softened
3 cups shredded rotisserie chicken
1 cup whipping cream
¼ cup freshly shredded Parmesan cheese
2 Tbsp. chopped fresh parsley
1 Tbsp. Italian dressing mix

1. Cook noodles according to package directions; drain well, and return noodles to pan.
2. Stir in 2 Tbsp. butter, and toss to coat. Stir in shredded chicken and remaining ingredients. Cook mixture over medium-high heat, tossing to coat evenly, 5 minutes or until thoroughly heated. Serve immediately.

Simple Swap

For added color and flavor, you can stir in steam-in-bag broccoli florets, prepared according to package directions.

Basic spaghetti and chicken get a speedy flavor overhaul with prepared Thai peanut sauce and fresh bell peppers.

Time-Saver

Pick up presliced peppers from the produce section to make this dish even faster.

Chicken Sesame Noodles

Makes 6 servings **Hands-on Time:** 10 min. **Total Time:** 20 min.

1 (14.5-oz.) package multigrain spaghetti
¾ cup Thai peanut sauce
3 green onions, sliced
½ red bell pepper, cut into strips
2 Tbsp. chopped fresh cilantro
1 Tbsp. fresh lime juice
3 cups sliced rotisserie chicken
1 Tbsp. sesame seeds, toasted

1. Prepare spaghetti according to package directions. Toss with peanut sauce, green onions, red bell pepper, cilantro, and lime juice. Stir in chicken. Sprinkle with toasted sesame seeds.

Note: We tested with House of Tsang Thai Peanut Sauce.

Grab and Go!

Serve this entrée with fresh or frozen edamame, cooked according to package directions. As a starter or side dish, these pods are ready in no time.

❑ *fresh or frozen edamame*

Chicken and Broccoli Cobbler

Makes 4 servings **Hands-on Time:** 16 min. **Total Time:** 46 min.

¼ cup butter, melted
5 oz. cubed sourdough
   bread (3 cups)
½ cup (2 oz.) grated
   Parmesan cheese
3 cups small broccoli florets
3 cups chopped rotisserie
   chicken

½ cup drained chopped
   roasted red bell pepper
1 (10-oz.) container
   refrigerated Alfredo
   sauce
½ cup sour cream
2 Tbsp. dry sherry

1. Preheat oven to 400°. Drizzle butter over bread cubes in a large bowl; sprinkle with cheese, and toss well.

2. Combine broccoli and next 5 ingredients in a large bowl. Spoon filling into a lightly greased 2-qt. rectangular or oval baking dish or individual baking dishes; top with bread cube mixture.

3. Bake, uncovered, at 400° for 30 minutes (20 to 25 minutes for individual cobblers) or until bubbly and top is toasted.

FROM THE KITCHEN

This savory cobbler can be made the night or morning before. Pop it in the oven when you get home, and your dinner will be ready in 30 minutes.

Crisp sourdough croutons, baked atop bubbling chicken, vegetables, and Alfredo sauce, are this casserole's crowning glory.

Time-Saver

You don't have to precook the broccoli for this delicious dish. Bagged broccoli florets from the produce section will be crisp-tender when this dish is done.

Bistro Grilled Chicken Pizza

The rectangular shape, grilled crust, and fun toppings like feta, fresh basil, and chicken make this pizza taste like something you would order at a restaurant!

Makes 6 servings **Hands-on Time:** 15 min. **Total Time:** 25 min.

1 (13.8-oz.) can refrigerated pizza crust dough
1 tsp. olive oil
¾ cup pizza sauce
4 plum tomatoes, sliced
2 cups chopped rotisserie chicken
1 (4-oz.) package tomato-and-basil feta cheese
1 cup (4 oz.) shredded mozzarella cheese
2 Tbsp. small fresh basil leaves

1. Preheat grill to 300° to 350° (medium) heat. Unroll dough, and place on a lightly greased 18- x 12-inch sheet of heavy-duty aluminum foil. Starting at center, press out dough with hands to form a 13- x 9-inch rectangle. Brush dough evenly with olive oil.

2. Invert dough onto grill cooking grate; peel off foil. Grill, covered with grill lid, 2 to 3 minutes or until bottom of dough is golden brown. Turn dough over, and grill, covered with grill lid, 1 to 2 minutes or until bottom is set. Carefully remove crust from grill to an aluminum foil-lined baking sheet.

3. Microwave pizza sauce in a small glass bowl at HIGH 30 seconds or until warm, stirring once. Spread sauce evenly over crust; top with tomatoes and chicken. Sprinkle evenly with cheeses. Return pizza to cooking grate (pizza should slide easily). Grill, covered with grill lid, 3 to 5 more minutes or until crust is done and cheese is melted. Sprinkle with basil leaves.

Time-Saver

Jarred pizza sauce and refrigerated crust dough make this a simple solution to a dinnertime rut. Leftover sauce will last even longer if kept in a plastic container in the freezer.

FROM THE KITCHEN

Use long-handled grilling tongs and a spatula to turn the dough with ease.

Buffalo Chicken Pizza

Makes 4 servings **Hands-on Time:** 6 min. **Total Time:** 16 min.

Vegetable cooking spray
½ cup Buffalo-style hot
   sauce
1 (16-oz.) package prebaked
   Italian pizza crust
2 cups chopped rotisserie
   chicken

1 cup (4 oz.) shredded
   provolone cheese
¼ cup crumbled blue
   cheese
1 Tbsp. chopped green
   onions

1. Coat cold cooking grate of grill with cooking spray, and place on grill. Preheat grill to 300° to 350° (medium) heat.
2. Spread hot sauce over crust, and layer with next 3 ingredients.
3. Place crust directly on cooking grate. Grill, covered with grill lid, 4 minutes. Rotate pizza one-quarter turn, and grill, covered with grill lid, 5 to 6 more minutes or until thoroughly heated. Sprinkle with green onions and serve immediately.

Note: We tested with Boboli prebaked pizza crust.

FROM THE KITCHEN
To make an oven-baked pizza instead, assemble pizza as directed, and bake according to package directions for pizza crust.

If you love Buffalo wings and you love pizza, this fun flavor combo over a grilled crust is sure to please.

Simple Swap

If your kids aren't fans of the heat in this recipe, you can use milder barbecue sauce in place of hot sauce.

Pesto Chicken Quesadillas

Makes 4 servings **Hands-on Time:** 12 min. **Total Time:** 20 min.

1 (3.5-oz.) jar prepared pesto
4 (8-inch) flour tortillas
1½ cups shredded rotisserie chicken

1 (8-oz.) package shredded Italian cheese blend
Butter, softened

1. Spread about 1½ Tbsp. pesto on each tortilla. Sprinkle a slightly heaping ⅓ cup chicken onto half of each tortilla; sprinkle cheese over chicken on each tortilla. Fold each tortilla in half. Butter both sides of each folded tortilla.
2. Heat a large nonstick skillet over medium-high heat. Cook quesadillas, in 2 batches, 2 minutes on each side or until browned and crusty. Remove to a cutting board, and cut each quesadilla into 3 wedges.

FROM THE KITCHEN

If you have a panini press, this would be the perfect use of it. Just spray press with cooking spray and cook each quesadilla for 2 minutes total.

Grab and Go!

You can serve these quick quesadillas with a simple salad for a quick-fix weeknight meal.

❑ *1 bag of salad*

❑ *1 bottle of your favorite dressing*

Instead of chips, these "nachos" have grilled red bell peppers to hold all the yummy toppings.

Pepper and Chicken "Nachos"

Makes 4 servings **Hands-on Time:** 12 min. **Total Time:** 37 min.

4 garlic cloves, pressed
¼ cup cider vinegar
⅓ cup olive oil
½ tsp. ground cumin
½ tsp. salt
½ tsp. freshly ground pepper
4 medium-size red bell peppers, cut into 2-inch pieces

2 cups chopped rotisserie chicken
1 (15½-oz.) can black-eyed peas, drained and rinsed
1 (8-oz.) pkg. shredded sharp Cheddar cheese
⅓ cup loosely packed fresh cilantro leaves

1. Preheat grill to 350° to 400° (medium-high) heat. Combine garlic and next 5 ingredients. Reserve 3 Tbsp. garlic mixture. Pour remaining garlic mixture into a large shallow dish; add peppers, turning to coat. Cover and chill 15 minutes, turning once. Remove peppers from marinade, reserving marinade for basting.

2. Grill peppers, covered with grill lid, 4 to 5 minutes or until grill marks appear and peppers are slightly tender, turning occasionally and basting with marinade.

3. Preheat broiler with oven rack 4 inches from heat. Combine chicken and peas with reserved 3 Tbsp. garlic mixture. Place peppers in a single layer on a lightly greased rack in an aluminum foil-lined broiler pan. Top each pepper with chicken mixture. Sprinkle peppers evenly with cheese.

4. Broil 4 to 5 minutes or until cheese is melted. Remove from oven, sprinkle with cilantro, and serve immediately.

Simple Swap

Feel free to use any type of canned beans in this recipe; black beans and cannellini beans would be two great alternatives.

Grab and Go!

Pick up a box of Spanish rice to round out this colorful and flavor-packed meal. Prepare according to package directions.

❏ *1 box Spanish rice*

Ranch House
Fettuccine

YOUR SECRET'S SAFE

from-scratch flavor in a fraction of the time

A little cumin and some key additions like hominy, chiles, and corn give this chicken and dressing recipe a Southwest kick.

Simple Swap

You can use sage stuffing mix instead of country-style stuffing and regular canned corn instead of cream-style corn.

Santa Fe Chicken and Dressing

Makes 4 to 6 servings **Hands-on Time:** 15 min. **Total Time:** 55 min.

4 cups cubed country-style stuffing
2 cups chopped rotisserie chicken
1 (15.5-oz.) can golden hominy, drained
1 (4.5-oz.) can chopped green chiles, drained
½ cup red bell pepper, chopped
½ cup minced fresh cilantro
1 (10¾-oz.) can cream of mushroom soup, undiluted
1 (8¾-oz.) can cream-style corn
1 cup sour cream
2 tsp. ground cumin
1 cup (4 oz.) shredded Monterey Jack cheese

1. Preheat oven to 350°. Combine first 6 ingredients in a large bowl; add soup and next 3 ingredients, stirring well. Spread in a lightly greased 2-qt. shallow baking dish.
2. Bake, covered, at 350° for 35 minutes or until thoroughly heated. Uncover and sprinkle with cheese; bake 5 more minutes or until cheese melts.

serve with
**Avocado Fruit
Salad**
page 136

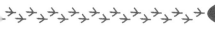

Quick-and-Easy King Ranch Chicken Casserole

Makes 8 to 10 servings **Hands-on Time:** 25 min.
Total Time: 1 hr., 30 min.

2 Tbsp. butter
1 medium onion, chopped
1 medium-size green bell pepper, chopped
1 garlic clove, pressed
¾ cup chicken broth
1 (10 ¾-oz.) can cream of mushroom soup
2 (10-oz.) cans diced tomatoes and green chiles, drained
1 (10 ¾-oz.) can cream of chicken soup
1 tsp. dried oregano
1 tsp. ground cumin
1 tsp. Mexican-style chili powder
3 cups shredded rotisserie chicken
3 cups (12 oz.) shredded sharp Cheddar cheese
3 cups coarsely crumbled lime-flavored white corn tortilla chips

1. Preheat oven to 350°. Melt butter in a large skillet over medium-high heat. Add onion, and sauté 6 to 7 minutes or until tender. Add bell pepper and garlic, and sauté 3 to 4 minutes. Stir in chicken broth, cream of mushroom soup, and next 5 ingredients. Cook, stirring occasionally, 8 minutes.
2. Layer half of chicken in a lightly greased 13- x 9-inch baking dish. Top with half of soup mixture and 1 cup Cheddar cheese. Cover with half of corn tortilla chips. Repeat layers once. Top with remaining 1 cup cheese.
3. Bake at 350° for 55 minutes to 1 hour or until bubbly. Let stand 10 minutes before serving.

You can't go wrong with a King Ranch Casserole! Our version is simplified with rotisserie chicken and flavored tortilla chips.

Simple Swap

Substitute 1 tsp. chili powder and ⅛ tsp. ground red pepper for Mexican-style chili powder, if desired.

editor's favorite

Chicken and Smoked Sausage Cassoulet

Makes 6 to 8 servings **Hands-on Time:** 15 min. **Total Time:** 53 min.

½ lb. smoked sausage, sliced
1 cup chopped onion
1 small butternut squash, peeled and cubed
2 cups shredded rotisserie chicken
1 (15.5-oz.) can cannellini beans, drained and rinsed
1 (14-oz.) can chicken broth

1 (14½-oz.) can diced tomatoes with rosemary and oregano, undrained
½ tsp. salt
¼ tsp. freshly ground pepper
2 cups soft, fresh breadcrumbs
3 Tbsp. butter, melted

1. Cook sausage in a large cast-iron or ovenproof skillet over medium-high heat, stirring often, 4 minutes or until browned. Remove sausage.

2. Sauté onion and squash in skillet 5 minutes or until onion is tender. Stir in sausage, chicken, and next 5 ingredients. Bring to a boil; cover, reduce heat, and simmer 25 minutes or until squash is tender.

3. Preheat broiler with oven rack 5½ inches from heat. Stir together breadcrumbs and butter; sprinkle over sausage mixture. Broil 1 minute or until breadcrumbs are lightly browned and crisp.

This smoky-sweet, hearty meal is the perfect fix for a chilly night.

FROM THE KITCHEN

To make the breadcrumbs in this recipe, pulse 4 to 5 slices firm white bread in a food processor until finely chopped. Measure 2 cups.

Chicken and Sweet Potato Pot Pie

Makes 6 to 8 servings **Hands-on Time:** 25 min.
Total Time: 1 hr., 30 min.

2 Tbsp. butter
1 (10-oz.) package frozen diced onion, red and green bell pepper, and celery
1½ cups peeled and diced sweet potato (about 1 large)
1 (10¾-oz.) can cream of chicken soup

3 cups chopped rotisserie chicken
1 cup frozen English peas
½ cup milk
2 tsp. chopped fresh thyme
¼ tsp. salt
¼ tsp. freshly ground pepper
1 (14.1-oz.) package refrigerated piecrusts

1. Preheat oven to 400°. Melt butter in a large Dutch oven over medium-high heat; add frozen vegetables and sweet potato. Sauté 10 minutes or until just tender. Stir in soup and next 6 ingredients.
2. Fit 1 piecrust into a 9-inch deep-dish pie plate according to package directions. Spoon chicken mixture into crust; place remaining piecrust over chicken mixture. Seal edges, and crimp. Cut slits in pastry to allow steam to escape.
3. Bake at 400° for 50 minutes or until crust is golden brown. Let stand 15 minutes before serving.

The thick, hearty filling in this pie makes for nice, clean slices. Be sure to seal the top and bottom crusts together so that the filling doesn't leak out.

FROM THE KITCHEN

To make this recipe in individual baking dishes, cut 3 rounds from each pie crust. Divide filling among 6 (10-oz.) ramekins. Top each with a piecrust round; seal, and flute. Cut slits in top crust, and bake at 400° for 35 to 40 minutes or until crust is golden brown.

serve with
Oven-Roasted Asparagus
page 132

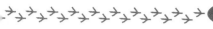
Double-Crust Chicken Pot Pie

Makes 6 to 8 servings **Hands-on Time:** 20 min.
Total Time: 1 hr., 30 min.

½ cup butter
2 medium leeks, sliced
½ cup all-purpose flour
1 (14-oz.) can chicken broth
3 cups chopped rotisserie
   chicken
1½ cups frozen cubed hash
   browns with onions and
   peppers
1 cup matchstick carrots
⅓ cup chopped fresh
   flat-leaf parsley
½ tsp. salt
½ tsp. freshly ground
   pepper
1 (17.3-oz.) package frozen
   puff pastry sheets,
   thawed
1 large egg

1. Preheat oven to 375°. Melt butter in a large skillet over medium heat; add leeks, and sauté 3 minutes. Sprinkle with flour; cook, stirring constantly, 3 minutes. Whisk in chicken broth; bring to a boil, whisking constantly. Remove from heat; stir in chicken and next 5 ingredients.

2. Roll each pastry sheet into a 12- x 10-inch rectangle on a lightly floured surface. Fit 1 sheet into a 9-inch deep-dish pie plate; spoon chicken mixture into pastry. Place remaining pastry sheet over filling in opposite direction of bottom sheet; fold edges under, and press with tines of a fork, sealing to bottom crust. Whisk together egg and 1 Tbsp. water, and brush over top of pie.

3. Bake at 375° on lower oven rack 55 to 60 minutes or until browned. Let stand 15 minutes.

This puff pastry crust bakes up very flaky, light, and golden, wowing your guests and family.

Simple Swap

Shredded hash browns can be used in place of cubed and still make a perfect pot pie.

Wide egg noodles create the perfect base for this rustic meal, soaking up all the flavorful juices.

FROM THE KITCHEN

Add depth and complexity to this rustic dish by using flavored diced tomatoes.

Chicken Cacciatore

Makes 4 servings **Hands-on Time:** 17 min. **Total Time:** 43 min.

1 rotisserie chicken
1 medium onion, sliced
1 red bell pepper, cut into strips
1 Tbsp. olive oil
½ cup dry red wine
½ tsp. salt
½ tsp. freshly ground pepper

2 (14.5-oz.) cans diced tomatoes with basil, garlic, and oregano, undrained
½ cup chicken broth
3 Tbsp. capers, drained

1. Skin chicken. Cut chicken, using kitchen shears, along both sides of backbone, separating the backbone from the chicken. Remove and discard backbone. Quarter chicken.

2. Sauté onion and bell pepper in hot oil in a large skillet over medium-high heat 8 minutes or until tender. Add wine, salt, and pepper; bring to a boil. Boil 1 minute or until liquid is reduced by half.

3. Add tomatoes, broth, and capers. Bring to a boil; cover, reduce heat, and simmer 10 minutes. Add chicken pieces. Cover and simmer 10 minutes or until chicken is thoroughly heated, turning pieces over after 5 minutes.

Try a new twist on traditional chicken and dumplings with the addition of paprika and chorizo sausage.

Simple Swap

If you can't find saffron, substitute ½ tsp. turmeric; it will give you that same golden color with a slightly more mustardy flavor.

Spanish Chicken and Dumplings

Makes 4 to 6 servings **Hands-on Time:** 8 min. **Total Time:** 35 min.

6 cups low-sodium fat-free chicken broth
½ tsp. saffron threads
4 oz. chorizo sausage or smoked sausage, diagonally sliced
½ cup chopped onion
1 (8-oz.) package baby portobello (crimini) mushrooms, quartered
1 tsp. fresh thyme leaves
¼ tsp. smoked paprika
1½ cups all-purpose baking mix
⅓ cup milk
2 cups shredded rotisserie chicken

1. Bring broth and saffron to a boil in a medium saucepan over medium heat. Remove from heat.
2. Cook sausage in a large Dutch oven over medium heat, stirring occasionally, 6 minutes or until browned. Remove sausage, reserving drippings in skillet. Drain sausage on paper towels.
3. Sauté onion and mushrooms in hot drippings 6 minutes or until onion is tender. Add broth mixture, thyme, and paprika; simmer 5 minutes.
4. Stir together baking mix and milk in a medium bowl with a fork just until dry ingredients are moistened. Turn dough out onto a floured surface, and knead 4 or 5 times. Roll dough to ⅛-inch thickness; cut into (1½- x 2½-inch) strips.
5. Bring broth mixture to a rolling boil. Drop dumplings, 1 at a time, into boiling broth mixture. Cover, reduce heat, and simmer 5 minutes, stirring occasionally. Stir in sausage and chicken; bring to a boil, and cook just until thoroughly heated. Let stand 5 minutes or until sauce slightly thickens.

Note: We tested with Bisquick Original Pancake and Baking Mix.

Chicken Corncakes

Makes 4 servings **Hands-on Time:** 15 min. **Total Time:** 15 min.

2 cups shredded rotisserie
 chicken
1 (8-oz.) can Mexican-style
 corn
1¼ cups panko (Japanese
 breadcrumbs)
1 cup (4 oz.) shredded
 sharp Cheddar cheese
1 Tbsp. finely chopped fresh
 chives

1 Tbsp. sour cream
½ tsp. salt
¼ tsp. freshly ground
 pepper
1 large egg
¼ cup olive oil
Toppings: salsa, sour
 cream, chopped fresh
 chives

1. Stir together chicken, corn, ¼ cup panko, cheese, and
next 5 ingredients in a large bowl. Shape mixture into
8 (3-inch) patties. Place remaining 1 cup panko in a shallow
dish. Dredge patties in panko, gently pressing to adhere.
2. Cook half of patties in 2 Tbsp. hot oil in a large skillet over
medium heat 2 to 3 minutes on each side or until golden.
Repeat procedure with remaining patties and oil. Serve with
desired toppings.

FROM THE KITCHEN
To make shaping the patties easier,
form the mixture for each patty
into a ball, and then flatten in your
hand. Carefully dredge in panko.

Wonderful as a light dinner, these loaded corncakes also work as a great 8-serving appetizer.

Who knew making chimichangas at home was this easy? Just load up your tortillas like a burrito, and fry for less than a minute.

Southwestern Chimichangas

Makes 6 servings **Hands-on Time:** 20 min. **Total Time:** 20 min.

½ cup frozen chopped spinach, thawed
1 (11-oz.) can Southwestern-style corn, drained
1 cup finely chopped rotisserie chicken
¼ cup chopped green onions
1 Tbsp. taco seasoning

6 (8-inch) soft taco-size flour tortillas
1 cup (4 oz.) shredded pepper Jack cheese
Peanut oil
Toppings: salsa, sour cream, chopped cilantro

1. Drain spinach well, pressing between paper towels.

2. Stir together spinach, corn, and next 3 ingredients in a medium-size, microwave-safe bowl. Microwave at HIGH 1 minute or until warm; stir well.

3. Warm tortillas in microwave according to package directions. Spoon about ½ cup chicken mixture just below center of each tortilla; sprinkle evenly with cheese. Fold opposite sides of tortilla over filling, and roll up. Secure with wooden picks. Flatten slightly with hand.

4. Pour peanut oil to a depth of 2 inches into a large heavy saucepan; heat to 375°. Fry chimichangas, in 3 batches, 30 seconds or just until golden brown; drain on paper towels. Serve with desired toppings. Remove wooden picks before serving.

Grab and Go!

Make these into a meal with a dollop of guacamole and a side of Mexican rice, prepared according to package directions.

❑ *1 package refrigerated guacamole*

❑ *1 box Mexican rice*

Ranch House Fettuccine

Makes 4 servings **Hands-on Time:** 20 min. **Total Time:** 20 min.

1 (8-oz.) package fettuccine
1 (16-oz.) package fresh broccoli florets
1 medium-size red bell pepper, diced
2 Tbsp. olive oil
1 garlic clove, minced
¾ cup cooked ham, cut into thin strips
2 cups chopped rotisserie chicken

4 sun-dried tomato halves in oil, drained and chopped
2 tsp. minced fresh rosemary
1 (8-oz.) bottle Ranch dressing
1 oz. shredded Parmesan cheese

1. Prepare pasta according to package directions. Drain and keep warm.

2. Sauté broccoli and bell pepper in hot oil in a large skillet over medium-high heat 7 minutes or until crisp-tender; add garlic, and sauté 2 minutes.

3. Stir in ham, chicken, and tomatoes; sprinkle with rosemary. Cook, stirring occasionally, until thoroughly heated.

4. Toss together warm pasta, broccoli mixture, and half of Ranch dressing. Sprinkle with cheese. Serve in bowls with remaining Ranch dressing.

This creamy fettuccine, loaded with veggies, ham, and chicken, is even better reheated the next day as a quick lunch or easy dinner.

Simple Swap

Try using a flavored Ranch dressing like spicy or bacon Ranch for an unexpected twist on this recipe.

Grab and Go!

Warm, crisp breadsticks are all you need to complete this delectable dish that's ready in less than 30 minutes.

❑ *breadsticks*

White Lightning
Chicken Chili

WARM & COMFORTING

heartwarming soups, stews, and gumbos

Easy Chicken and Dumplings

Makes 4 to 6 servings **Hands-on Time:** 15 min. **Total Time:** 40 min.

1 (32-oz.) container
   low-sodium fat-free
   chicken broth
3 cups shredded rotisserie
   chicken
1 (10¾-oz.) can reduced-fat
   cream of chicken soup
¼ tsp. poultry seasoning
1 (10-oz.) can refrigerated
   buttermilk biscuits
2 carrots, diced
3 celery ribs, diced

1. Bring first 4 ingredients to a boil in a Dutch oven over medium-high heat. Cover, reduce heat to low, and simmer, stirring occasionally, 5 minutes. Increase heat to medium-high; return to a low boil.

2. Place biscuits on a lightly floured surface. Roll or pat each biscuit to ⅛-inch thickness; cut into ½-inch-wide strips.

3. Drop strips, 1 at a time, into boiling broth mixture. Add carrots and celery. Cover, reduce heat to low, and simmer 15 to 20 minutes, stirring occasionally to prevent dumplings from sticking.

Our version of this Southern comfort food is made quick and easy with refrigerated buttermilk biscuits and cream of chicken soup.

FROM THE KITCHEN

Stirring the chicken and dumplings as they simmer is crucial for keeping your delicious dumplings from sticking together.

Time-Saver

This recipe is great for busy cooks who want homemade flavor, since most of the ingredients are common kitchen staples kept on hand.

Cozy up with this rich and velvety broccoli chicken soup.

Creamy Chicken Divan Soup

Makes 12 servings **Hands-on Time:** 30 min. **Total Time:** 50 min.

2 Tbsp. butter
1 medium-size sweet onion, chopped
1 garlic clove, chopped
¼ tsp. dried crushed red pepper
1 (48-oz.) container chicken broth
2 (12-oz.) packages fresh broccoli florets

1 (8-oz.) package cream cheese, cut into cubes
4 cups chopped rotisserie chicken
1 (8-oz.) block sharp Cheddar cheese, shredded
Salt and pepper to taste
Garnishes: cracked black pepper, chopped chives

1. Melt butter in a Dutch oven over medium-high heat; add onion, and sauté 5 to 6 minutes or until tender. Add garlic and red pepper, and cook 2 minutes. Stir in chicken broth and broccoli. Cover and bring to a boil; reduce heat to medium, and cook 10 to 15 minutes or until broccoli is tender. Stir in cream cheese.
2. Process mixture with a handheld blender until smooth. Add chicken and shredded cheese. Cook, stirring occasionally, 5 minutes or until cheese is melted. Season with salt and pepper to taste. Serve immediately. Garnish, if desired.

Simple Swap

Try other fun toppings, such as crumbled cooked bacon, green onions, or a dash of hot sauce.

FROM THE KITCHEN

If you don't have a handheld immersion blender, let the mixture cool slightly; process the mixture, in batches, in a regular blender until smooth, stopping to scrape down the sides as needed. Return the mixture to the Dutch oven, and proceed as directed.

This soup is even better the next day and freezes well for a go-to dish on hectic weeknights.

Simple Swap

Feel free to use any of your favorite mushrooms in this hearty chicken-and-rice soup. Some of our favorites are crimini, chanterelle, and shiitake mushrooms.

FROM THE KITCHEN

For thinner soup, reduce the amount of flour to ¼ cup.

Chicken, Mushroom, and Wild Rice Soup

Makes 14 servings **Hands-on Time:** 30 min. **Total Time:** 40 min.

2 (6.2-oz.) boxes
   fast-cooking long-grain
   and wild rice mix
10 cups chicken broth,
   divided
3 Tbsp. butter
1 cup sliced fresh
   mushrooms
1 cup chopped onion
1 cup chopped celery

¼ cup butter
½ cup all-purpose flour
½ cup half-and-half
2 Tbsp. dry white wine
2 cups shredded rotisserie
   chicken
Garnishes: fresh parsley
   leaves, freshly ground
   pepper

1. Bring rice, 1 seasoning packet from rice mix, and 4 cups chicken broth to a boil in a saucepan over medium-high heat. Cover, reduce heat to low, and simmer 20 minutes or until liquid is absorbed and rice is tender. (Reserve remaining seasoning packet for another use.)
2. Meanwhile, melt 3 Tbsp. butter in a large skillet over medium heat; add mushrooms, onion, and celery, and cook, stirring often, 10 to 12 minutes or until tender.
3. Melt ¼ cup butter in a Dutch oven over medium heat; whisk in flour, and cook, whisking constantly, 1 minute, or until thickened and bubbly. Gradually whisk in remaining 6 cups broth, and cook, stirring often, 8 to 10 minutes or until slightly thickened. Whisk in half-and-half and wine. Stir in mushroom mixture, chicken, and rice. Cook, stirring occasionally, 5 to 10 minutes or until thoroughly heated. (Do not boil.) Garnish, if desired.

serve with
**Cheddar
Drop Biscuits**
page 165

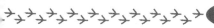
Chicken-Kale Soup

Makes 7 servings **Hands-on Time:** 15 min. **Total Time:** 35 min.

2 tsp. olive oil
1 cup chopped onion
3 garlic cloves, minced
6 cups coarsely chopped
    packed kale (about
    5 oz.)
½ cup dry white wine or
    low-sodium fat-free
    chicken broth

6 cups low-sodium fat-free
    chicken broth
2 cups chopped skinless
    rotisserie chicken breast
½ cup uncooked long-grain
    rice
1 tsp. fresh thyme leaves
¼ tsp. salt
1 bay leaf

1. Heat oil in a Dutch oven over medium heat. Add onion
and garlic; sauté 7 minutes or until tender and lightly
browned. Add kale; sauté 2 minutes or just until kale wilts.
Add wine; cook 1 minute. Add 6 cups broth and remaining
ingredients; bring to a boil.
2. Cover, reduce heat, and simmer 20 minutes or until rice is
tender. Discard bay leaf before serving.

Simple Swap

To add some whole grain to this soup, substitute
uncooked brown rice for the long-grain rice.

If you've never tried kale, this comforting chicken-and-rice soup will make you fall in love with this mild, slightly bitter green vegetable.

Chunky Chicken-Barley Soup

Makes 4 servings **Hands-on Time:** 10 min. **Total Time:** 45 min.

2 tsp. olive oil
1 cup chopped onion
1 cup chopped carrot
½ cup chopped celery
2 garlic cloves, minced
2 (14-oz.) cans low-sodium
    fat-free chicken broth

¼ tsp. salt
¼ tsp. dried thyme
¼ tsp. pepper
1 cup chopped rotisserie
    chicken
½ cup uncooked
    quick-cooking barley

1. Sauté first 4 ingredients in hot oil in a large Dutch oven over medium-high heat 5 minutes. Add chicken broth, 1¾ cups water, and next 3 ingredients. Bring to a boil; reduce heat, and simmer, partially covered, 23 to 25 minutes or until vegetables are tender.
2. Add chicken and barley; cook 8 to 10 minutes or until barley is tender.

FROM THE KITCHEN

Comfort food at its best, this hearty soup recipe can be doubled and kept in the freezer for a quick make-ahead meal to enjoy more than once.

Grab and Go!

Pick up some dinner rolls from the freezer section to complement this soup. A simple grilled cheese sandwich is another great option that your kids will appreciate.

❑ *frozen dinner rolls*

FROM THE KITCHEN

By buying cans of flavored beans, corn, and tomatoes, you need fewer ingredients and are letting the store do most of the work for you.

Fiesta Chicken Soup

Makes 8 servings **Hands-on Time:** 10 min. **Total Time:** 30 min.

1 medium onion, diced
1 tsp. vegetable oil
1 garlic clove, minced
3 cups chopped rotisserie chicken
1 (15-oz.) can chili-hot beans, undrained
3½ cups chicken broth
1 (15¼-oz.) can whole kernel corn with red and green peppers, drained
1 (10-oz.) can diced tomatoes and green chiles, undrained
½ tsp. chili powder
½ tsp. ground cumin
⅛ tsp. salt
⅛ tsp. pepper
Toppings: sour cream, shredded Mexican four-cheese blend

1. Sauté onion in hot oil in a large Dutch oven over medium heat 7 minutes or until tender. Add garlic, and sauté 1 minute. Stir in chicken and next 8 ingredients.
2. Bring to a boil, stirring occasionally; reduce heat, and simmer 15 minutes. Serve with desired toppings.

Grab and Go!

Your kids will love this hearty soup with a kick of Mexican flavor. Serve with cheesy breadsticks.

❑ *cheese-topped breadsticks*

serve with
**Sour Cream
Cornsticks**
page 171

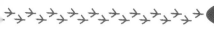
White Lightning Chicken Chili

Makes 10 servings **Hands-on Time:** 10 min. **Total Time:** 25 min.

1 large sweet onion, diced
2 garlic cloves, minced
2 Tbsp. olive oil
4 cups shredded rotisserie chicken
2 (14-oz.) cans chicken broth
2 (4.5-oz.) cans chopped green chiles, undrained
1 (1.25-oz.) envelope white chicken chili seasoning mix

3 (15-oz.) cans navy beans, undrained
Toppings: Avocado-Mango Salsa, sour cream, shredded Monterey Jack cheese, fresh cilantro leaves

1. Sauté onion and garlic in hot oil in a large Dutch oven over medium-high heat 5 minutes or until onion is tender. Stir in chicken, next 3 ingredients, and 2 cans navy beans. Coarsely mash remaining can navy beans, and stir into chicken mixture.
2. Bring to a boil, stirring often; cover, reduce heat to medium-low, and simmer, stirring occasionally, 10 minutes. Serve with desired toppings.

Avocado-Mango Salsa

Stir together 1 large **avocado,** cubed; 1 cup diced **fresh mango;** ⅓ cup diced **red onion;** 2 Tbsp. chopped **fresh cilantro;** and 2 Tbsp. **fresh lime juice.** Serve immediately. Makes 2 cups.

This speedy chicken and white bean chili is brightened with a spoonful of easy Avocado-Mango Salsa on top.

FROM THE KITCHEN

Don't be tempted to drain the green chiles or navy beans; the liquid gives this chili extra body and flavor.

Simple Swap

If you like your gumbo spicy, feel free to add a little extra Creole seasoning for that kick you crave.

Big Easy Gumbo

Makes 8 to 10 servings **Hands-on Time:** 20 min. **Total Time:** 45 min.

½ cup peanut oil
½ cup all-purpose flour
1 cup chopped sweet onion
1 cup chopped green bell pepper
1 cup chopped celery
2 tsp. Creole seasoning
2 tsp. minced garlic
3 (14-oz.) cans low-sodium fat-free chicken broth

4 cups shredded rotisserie chicken
½ lb. andouille sausage, cut into ¼-inch-thick slices
1½ cups frozen black-eyed peas, thawed
1 lb. peeled, large raw shrimp (16/20 count)

1. Heat oil in a large Dutch oven over medium-high heat; gradually whisk in flour, and cook, whisking constantly, 5 to 7 minutes or until flour is chocolate colored. (Do not burn mixture.)

2. Reduce heat to medium. Stir in onion and next 4 ingredients, and cook, stirring constantly, 3 minutes. Gradually stir in chicken broth; add chicken and next 2 ingredients. Increase heat to medium-high, and bring to a boil. Reduce heat to low, and simmer, stirring occasionally, 20 minutes. Add shrimp, and cook 5 minutes or just until shrimp turn pink.

Note: We tested with Zatarain's Creole Seasoning and Savoie's Andouille Sausage.

Grab and Go!

Serve this Cajun classic with a loaf of French bread and a scoop of white rice, prepared according to package directions, for a dinner that's straight out of the Crescent City.

❑ *French bread*

❑ *1 (5.3-oz.) bag boil-in-bag rice*

Brunswick Stew

Makes 8 to 10 servings **Hands-on Time:** 5 min. **Total Time:** 30 min.

3 cups chicken broth
2 cups chopped rotisserie
    chicken
1 (24-oz.) container
    barbecued shredded
    pork
1 (16-oz.) package frozen
    vegetable gumbo
    mixture
1 (10-oz.) package frozen
    corn
½ (10-oz.) package frozen
    petite lima beans
½ cup ketchup

1. Bring all ingredients to a boil in a Dutch oven over medium-high heat, stirring often. Cover, reduce heat to low, and simmer, stirring occasionally, 25 minutes or until thoroughly heated.

This savory Southern stew will keep you warm as the nights cool down.

FROM THE KITCHEN

Double and freeze this recipe for a delicious dinner option you can simply thaw and heat up on busy weeknights.

Grab and Go!

Garnish with freshly ground pepper, and serve with fresh country-style bread from the bakery section of your local grocery.

❑ *sliced country-style bread*
❑ *freshly ground pepper*

Mexican Lime-Chicken Soup

Makes 8 servings **Hands-on Time:** 18 min. **Total Time:** 33 min.

2 Tbsp. vegetable oil
1 large red bell pepper, chopped
1 large onion, chopped
1 tsp. jarred minced garlic
2 (14½-oz.) cans Mexican-style stewed tomatoes, drained and chopped
2 limes
7 cups chicken broth
3 cups chopped rotisserie chicken
¼ cup fresh cilantro
1 Tbsp. chopped pickled jalapeño pepper
¼ tsp. salt
¼ tsp. freshly ground pepper
Toppings: shredded pepper Jack cheese, sour cream, lime wedges

1. Heat oil in a Dutch oven over medium-high heat. Add bell pepper, onion, and garlic; sauté 3 minutes or until vegetables are tender. Stir in tomatoes, and cook 2 minutes. Cut limes in half crosswise. Squeeze lime juice directly into vegetable mixture; add lime shells and chicken broth to soup. Bring to a boil; reduce heat, and simmer 10 minutes.
2. Remove and discard lime shells. Stir in chicken, cilantro, jalapeño, salt, and pepper. Cook 5 minutes or until thoroughly heated. Serve with toppings, if desired.

Grab and Go!

Tortilla chips are a tasty topping that adds delicious crunch to this soup. You can also top with avocado slices.

- ❑ *tortilla chips*
- ❑ *1 avocado, sliced*

Chicken Salad with Fresh
Peaches and Blue Cheese

LUNCH BREAK

crisp salads, melty paninis, and piled-high sandwiches

Tomato-Chicken Salad

Makes 4 servings **Hands-on Time:** 10 min. **Total Time:** 20 min.

1 lemon
2 lb. assorted tomatoes, halved or chopped
3 cups chopped rotisserie chicken
1 large English cucumber, sliced
½ cup chopped fresh flat-leaf parsley
¼ cup sliced green onions
¼ cup loosely packed fresh basil leaves
2 Tbsp. olive oil
1 tsp. salt
½ tsp. freshly ground pepper
½ cup crumbled feta cheese

1. Grate zest from lemon to equal 2 tsp.; squeeze juice from lemon to equal 2 Tbsp.
2. Combine lemon zest, juice, tomatoes, and next 8 ingredients in a large bowl. Lct stand 10 minutes. Toss with crumbled feta just before serving.

FROM THE KITCHEN

To keep the flavor of the feta at its best, don't add it to the salad until just before you serve it.

Grab and Go!

For an easy side dish, preheat your grill to 400° to 450° (high) heat. Brush 6 (1-inch-thick) ciabatta or French bread baguette slices with extra virgin olive oil. Grill bread 1 to 2 minutes on each side until toasted.

❑ *sliced bakery ciabatta or French bread*

FROM THE KITCHEN

This chicken salad is best eaten the day it's made, but it will last in the fridge for up to 3 days.

Chicken-Horseradish Salad

Makes 5 servings **Hands-on Time:** 10 min.
Total Time: 2 hr., 10 min.

3 cups chopped rotisserie chicken
2 celery ribs, chopped
⅔ cup light mayonnaise
½ cup green onions, minced
½ cup chopped pecans, toasted

2 to 3 Tbsp. refrigerated horseradish
2 tsp. fresh lemon juice
½ tsp. grated lemon zest
½ tsp. pepper
¼ tsp. salt

1. Stir together all ingredients in a large bowl. Cover and chill at least 2 hours before serving.

Grab and Go!

You can enjoy this twist on traditional chicken salad by itself, as a sandwich, or with assorted crackers for portable perfection.

❑ *assorted crackers*

Layer upon layer of crunch and flavor stack up to make this eye-catching salad that's great for entertaining.

Simple Swap

To make individual servings, divide ingredients among 4 (12-oz) glass dishes; layer as directed.

Chicken, Apple, and Smoked Gouda Salad

Makes 4 servings **Hands-on Time:** 20 min. **Total Time:** 20 min.

2 large Gala apples, thinly sliced (about 1 lb.)
2 Tbsp. fresh lemon juice
1 (5.5-oz.) package spring greens and baby spinach mix
3 cups shredded rotisserie chicken
1 small red onion, halved and sliced

1½ cups (6 oz.) shredded smoked Gouda cheese
1½ cups thinly sliced celery
1 cup sweetened dried cranberries
1 cup salted roasted pecans
1 cup bottled honey-mustard dressing

1. Toss apple slices with lemon juice.
2. Layer salad greens, apples, chicken, and next 5 ingredients in a large glass bowl. Serve immediately, or cover and chill up to 8 hours. Serve with dressing.

Waldorf Chicken Salad

Makes 6 servings **Hands-on Time:** 12 min. **Total Time:** 18 min.

½ cup chopped walnuts
3 cups chopped rotisserie
  chicken
1 cup seedless red grapes,
  halved

1 large Gala apple, diced
1 cup diced celery
½ cup mayonnaise
½ cup honey mustard
Salt and pepper to taste

1. Preheat oven to 350°. Bake walnuts in a single layer in a shallow pan 6 to 8 minutes or until toasted and fragrant, stirring halfway through.

2. Stir together chicken, next 5 ingredients, and walnuts. Add salt and pepper to taste.

Simple Swap

You can substitute pecans for walnuts, keeping the crunch while providing a new twist on this classic recipe.

Grab and Go!

Serve this salad over a bed of greens with a fresh bakery baguette for a lunchtime stunner.

❑ *bag of greens*

❑ *fresh bakery baguette*

serve with
**Broccoli-
Cornbread
Muffins**
page 173

Chicken Salad with Fresh Peaches and Blue Cheese

Fresh peaches and blue cheese put a Southern spin on ordinary chicken salad.

Makes 6 servings **Hands-on Time:** 10 min. **Total Time:** 10 min.

3 Tbsp. white wine vinegar
3 Tbsp. orange juice
1 Tbsp. honey
¼ tsp. kosher salt
¼ tsp. freshly ground
    pepper
2 Tbsp. extra virgin olive oil
6 cups chopped romaine
    lettuce

3 cups shredded rotisserie
    chicken
2 cups sliced peeled
    peaches (about
    2 medium)
½ cup crumbled blue
    cheese
¼ cup coarsely chopped
    smoked almonds

1. Combine first 5 ingredients in a small bowl. Add olive oil, and stir with a whisk.

2. Combine lettuce and next 4 ingredients in a large bowl, and toss gently. Drizzle with vinaigrette; toss to coat.

FROM THE KITCHEN

If you want to assemble this salad ahead, just keep it covered and chilled, and drizzle with vinaigrette just before serving.

Time-Saver

Using bagged chopped lettuce from the produce section speeds up prep time.

Vegetable Patch Chicken Salad

Makes 4 servings **Hands-on Time:** 10 min. **Total Time:** 40 min.

3 cups chopped rotisserie chicken
½ cup bottled cucumber-Ranch dressing
½ cup frozen tiny green sweet peas, thawed
¼ cup seeded, chopped cucumber

2 Tbsp. minced onion
2 Tbsp. minced red bell pepper
2 Tbsp. minced fresh parsley
1 Tbsp. fresh lemon juice

1. Stir together all ingredients in a large bowl. Cover and chill at least 30 minutes before serving.

Grab and Go!

To complete this lunchtime treat, serve it with assorted crackers.

❑ *assorted crackers*

Chicken Pan Bagnat

Makes 4 servings **Hands-on Time:** 12 min. **Total Time:** 12 min.

2 cups sliced skinless rotisserie chicken breast
1 cup thinly sliced zucchini
½ cup thinly sliced red onion
2 Tbsp. coarsely chopped pitted kalamata olives
¼ tsp. lemon zest
1½ tsp. fresh lemon juice
1½ tsp. olive oil
1 tsp. capers, drained and coarsely chopped

½ tsp. freshly ground pepper
¼ tsp. salt
¼ tsp. chopped fresh rosemary
1 (8-oz.) French bread baguette
4 small green leaf lettuce leaves
1 tomato, cut into 8 (¼-inch-thick) slices

1. Combine first 11 ingredients in a medium bowl; toss well. Set aside.

2. Cut baguette in half horizontally. Hollow out top and bottom halves of loaf, leaving a ½-inch border. Reserve torn bread for another use.

3. Arrange lettuce and tomato on bottom half of loaf. Spoon chicken mixture evenly over lettuce and tomato. Replace top half of loaf; cut crosswise into 4 equal portions.

This Provençal sandwich gets its name from the light dressing that flavors the chicken mixture and the baguette.

FROM THE KITCHEN

To make ahead, wrap tightly in plastic wrap and chill up to 2 hours.

Grab and Go!

This snazzy sandwich makes a delicious and satisfying lunch with a side of potato chips.

❏ *your favorite potato chips*

Simple Swap

If you don't have cooked bacon on hand, use refrigerated bacon bits for the same savory flavor.

Ranch Chicken Pita Pockets

Makes 4 servings **Hands-on Time:** 7 min. **Total Time:** 10 min.

2 cups shredded romaine
    lettuce
1½ cups shredded rotisserie
    chicken breast
1 cup chopped tomato
    (about 2 medium)

4 center-cut bacon slices,
    cooked and crumbled
⅓ cup light Ranch dressing
4 whole wheat pitas,
    warmed and halved

1. Combine first 4 ingredients in a bowl. Add dressing; toss well. Spoon lettuce mixture evenly into pita halves.

Grab and Go!

Pick up some baby carrots or celery sticks from the produce section to pair with these pitas.

❑ *baby carrots or celery sticks*

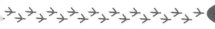
Hot Brown Panini

Makes 8 servings **Hands-on Time:** 16 min. **Total Time:** 24 min.

2 Tbsp. melted butter
16 (½-inch-thick) Italian bread slices
1 cup (4 oz.) shredded Swiss cheese, divided
3 cups chopped rotisserie chicken
4 plum tomatoes, sliced
3 cups warm White Cheese Sauce, divided
13 cooked bacon slices, crumbled

1. Preheat panini press.
2. Brush melted butter evenly on 1 side of each of 16 bread slices. Place, buttered sides down, on wax paper.
3. Sprinkle 1 Tbsp. Swiss cheese on top of each of 8 bread slices; top evenly with chicken, tomato slices, and 1 cup warm White Cheese Sauce. Sprinkle with bacon and remaining cheese, and top with remaining bread slices, buttered sides up.
4. Cook sandwiches, in batches, in a preheated panini press 2 to 3 minutes or until golden brown. Serve with remaining 2 cups warm White Cheese Sauce for dipping.

White Cheese Sauce

Melt ¼ cup **butter** in a heavy saucepan over low heat; whisk in ¼ cup **all-purpose flour** until smooth. Cook 1 minute, whisking constantly. Gradually whisk in 3½ cups **milk;** cook over medium heat, whisking constantly, until mixture is thickened and bubbly. Whisk in 1 cup (4 oz.) **shredded Swiss cheese** and 1 cup **grated Parmesan cheese,** ½ tsp. **salt,** and ¼ tsp. **ground red pepper,** whisking until cheeses melt and sauce is smooth. Makes 3 cups.

FROM THE KITCHEN

If you don't have a panini press, you can use a skillet or countertop grill to achieve delicious results.

Simple Swap

For a tasty twist on this panini, try using shredded provolone cheese instead of Swiss.

Chicken Salad Croissants

Makes 10 servings **Hands-on Time:** 15 min. **Total Time:** 45 min.

½ cup mayonnaise
½ cup sour cream
1 Tbsp. chopped fresh
   tarragon
½ tsp. salt
½ tsp. pepper
1½ cups chopped rotisserie
   chicken

½ cup seedless red grapes,
   halved
⅓ cup pecans, toasted and
   coarsely chopped
10 croissants
10 red leaf lettuce leaves

1. Stir together mayonnaise and next 4 ingredients in a large bowl. Add chicken, grapes, and chopped pecans, tossing to coat. Cover and chill at least 30 minutes.

2. Cut a slit horizontally on 1 side of each croissant; fill evenly with lettuce leaves and chicken salad. Secure with wooden picks.

FROM THE KITCHEN

To make ahead, prepare these sandwiches through Step 1, cover, and chill until ready to assemble and serve.

Time-Saver

You can easily double this recipe for crowd-pleasing party food. To save time, purchase croissants from the bakery section of your local market.

Chicken and Fontina Panini

Makes 2 servings **Hands-on Time:** 7 min. **Total Time:** 10 min.

1 (8-oz.) loaf ciabatta bread, cut in half horizontally
3 Tbsp. pesto sauce
2 plum tomatoes, sliced
1 cup shredded rotisserie chicken
2 slices fontina cheese

1. Preheat panini press.
2. Spread bottom half of bread with pesto. Top with tomato slices, chicken, and cheese. Top with bread.
3. Place sandwich in panini press; cook 3 to 4 minutes or until cheese melts and bread is toasted. Cut into quarters, and serve hot.

Grab and Go!

These made-to-order paninis are great for all seasons. Serve them with your favorite tomato soup or fresh fruit.

❑ *tomato soup*

❑ *fresh fruit*

kid-friendly

Simple Swap

Try using sharp Cheddar slices in place of Monterey Jack for an even more flavorful variation on these savory sandwiches.

Grilled Chicken and Cheese Sandwiches

Makes 6 servings **Hands-on Time:** 10 min. **Total Time:** 20 min.

2 cups chopped rotisserie
    chicken
⅓ cup golden raisins
¼ cup slivered almonds,
    toasted
¼ cup diced celery
½ cup mayonnaise

12 (¾-oz.) Monterey Jack
    cheese slices
12 whole wheat bread
    slices
¼ cup butter or margarine,
    softened

1. Stir together first 5 ingredients. Place 1 cheese slice on each of 6 bread slices; spread evenly with chicken mixture, and top with remaining cheese and bread slices. Spread half of butter evenly on 1 side of each sandwich.

2. Cook 3 sandwiches, buttered sides down, in a nonstick skillet or grill pan over medium heat 2 to 3 minutes or until lightly browned. Spread remaining butter evenly on ungrilled sides; turn and cook 3 minutes or until lightly browned. Repeat with remaining sandwiches.

FROM THE KITCHEN To toast the almonds, simply place them in a shallow baking pan and bake at 350° for 8 to 10 minutes.

Chicken
Stir-Fry

ACCENT ON FLAVOR

main dishes with international flair

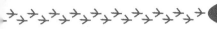
Greek Pizza with Chicken and Artichokes

Makes 4 servings **Hands-on Time:** 10 min. **Total Time:** 15 min.

1 (16-oz.) pkg. refrigerated pizza dough
1½ cups (6 oz.) shredded mozzarella cheese, divided
2 cups shredded rotisserie chicken
1 (7-oz.) jar roasted red bell peppers, drained and cut into strips
1 (6-oz.) jar marinated artichoke hearts, drained and coarsely chopped
10 kalamata olives, drained, pitted, and thinly sliced
1½ Tbsp. chopped fresh oregano
1 Tbsp. olive oil
½ tsp. freshly ground pepper
1 cup crumbled feta cheese

1. Preheat oven to 500°.
2. On a floured surface, roll out pizza dough to a 15-inch circle. Sprinkle ¾ cup mozzarella cheese onto prepared pizza dough. Top evenly with chicken.
3. Combine roasted red bell peppers and next 5 ingredients in a bowl; toss gently. Spoon mixture evenly over chicken. Sprinkle with remaining ¾ cup mozzarella cheese; top with feta cheese.
4. Bake at 500° for 5 to 7 minutes or until browned and bubbly.

Grab and Go!

Serve with a fresh green salad and your favorite Italian dressing for a simple side dish.

❑ bagged salad
❑ 1 bottle Italian dressing

Chicken-and-Green Chile Enchiladas

Makes 4 to 6 servings **Hands-on Time:** 20 min. **Total Time:** 50 min.

1 cup chopped onion
1 Tbsp. oil
1 tsp. jarred minced garlic
3½ cups chopped
    rotisserie chicken
2 (4.5-oz.) cans chopped
    green chiles, drained
1 Tbsp. chopped fresh
    cilantro

3 (10-oz.) cans enchilada
    sauce, divided
2 cups (8 oz.) shredded
    Mexican four-cheese
    blend, divided
8 (10-inch) burrito-size
    flour tortillas

1. Preheat oven to 425°. Sauté onion in hot oil in a 3½-qt. saucepan over medium heat 8 minutes or until tender; add garlic, and sauté 2 minutes.

2. Stir together onion mixture, chicken, chiles, cilantro, 1½ cups enchilada sauce, and 1 cup cheese.

3. Spoon about ½ cup chicken mixture down center of each tortilla; roll up tortillas, and place, seam sides down, in a lightly greased 13- x 9-inch baking dish. Pour remaining enchilada sauce over tortillas. Sprinkle with remaining 1 cup cheese.

4. Bake, covered, at 425° for 20 minutes; uncover and bake 10 more minutes or until cheese melts and is golden brown.

These saucy and cheesy enchiladas are just mildly spicy with the addition of canned green chiles. Turn up the heat by adding some chopped jalapeños!

Chicken Stir-Fry

Makes 4 to 6 servings **Hands-on Time:** 10 min. **Total Time:** 10 min.

1 (14-oz.) can low-sodium
  fat-free chicken broth
¼ cup lite soy sauce
1 to 2 Tbsp. chili-garlic
  sauce
2 Tbsp. cornstarch
1 Tbsp. brown sugar

1 tsp. ground ginger
2 Tbsp. dark sesame oil
3 cups shredded rotisserie
  chicken
1 (16-oz.) package frozen
  stir-fry vegetables

1. Whisk together first 6 ingredients.
2. Heat sesame oil in a large skillet or wok at medium-high heat 2 minutes. Add chicken and vegetables, and stir-fry 5 to 7 minutes. Add broth mixture, and stir-fry 1 to 2 minutes or until sauce thickens and vegetables are tender.

FROM THE KITCHEN

This dish is just as flavorful the next day. Pack it up with some white rice for a quick portable lunch.

Grab and Go!

Serve this quick entrée over instant rice or toss with cooked rice noodles.

❏ *instant white rice*

Mediterranean Chicken Couscous

Makes 8 servings **Hands-on Time:** 7 min. **Total Time:** 12 min.

1¼ cups low-sodium fat-free chicken broth
1 (5.6-oz.) package toasted pine nut-couscous mix
3 cups chopped rotisserie chicken
¼ cup chopped fresh basil
1 (4-oz.) package crumbled feta cheese

1 pt. grape tomatoes, halved
1 tsp. lemon zest
1½ Tbsp. fresh lemon juice
¼ tsp. pepper
Garnish: fresh basil leaves

1. Microwave broth and seasoning packet from couscous in a microwave-safe bowl at HIGH 2 to 3 minutes or until broth begins to boil. Place couscous in a large bowl, and stir in broth mixture. Cover and let stand 5 minutes.
2. Fluff couscous with a fork; stir in chicken and next 6 ingredients. Serve warm or cold. Garnish, if desired.

Simple Swap

Toss in chopped artichoke hearts and pitted kalamata olives for extra Mediterranean flavor.

Chicken Marsala Tetrazzini

Makes 6 to 8 servings **Hands-on Time:** 10 min. **Total Time:** 45 min.

1 (8-oz.) package vermicelli
2 Tbsp. butter
1 (8-oz.) package sliced
   fresh mushrooms
3 oz. finely chopped
   prosciutto
3 cups chopped rotisserie
   chicken
1 cup frozen English peas,
   thawed

1 (10¾-oz.) can
   reduced-fat cream
   of mushroom soup
1 (10-oz.) container
   refrigerated light
   Alfredo sauce
½ cup chicken broth
¼ cup Marsala
1 cup (4 oz.) shredded
   Parmesan cheese

1. Preheat oven to 350°. Prepare pasta according to package directions. Meanwhile, melt butter in a large skillet over medium-high heat; add mushrooms and prosciutto, and sauté 5 minutes.

2. Stir together mushroom mixture, chicken, next 5 ingredients, and ½ cup cheese; stir in pasta. Spoon mixture into a lightly greased 11- x 7-inch baking dish; sprinkle with remaining ½ cup cheese.

3. Bake at 350° for 35 minutes or until bubbly.

Simple Swap

While chopped prosciutto adds great savory flavor to this dish, it can easily be replaced with chopped bacon.

Grab and Go!

Round out this comforting casserole with a simple salad of chopped romaine lettuce, Caesar dressing, and croutons.

- ❑ *chopped romaine lettuce*
- ❑ *Caesar dressing*
- ❑ *croutons*

Served with toasted garlic bread and a simple salad, this Italian feast is a complete meal.

FROM THE KITCHEN

For an easy weeknight fix, double the recipe, and freeze half for another night. Prepare through Step 5 before freezing, and thaw well before baking.

Chicken and Spinach Pasta Bake

Makes 4 to 6 servings **Hands-on Time:** 15 min.
Total Time: 1 hr., 15 min.

8 oz. uncooked rigatoni
1 Tbsp. olive oil
1 cup finely chopped onion (about 1 medium)
1 (10-oz.) package frozen chopped spinach, thawed
3 cups chopped rotisserie chicken
1 (14½-oz.) can Italian-style diced tomatoes
1 (8-oz.) container chive-and-onion cream cheese
½ tsp. salt
½ tsp. pepper
1½ cups (6 oz.) shredded mozzarella cheese

1. Preheat oven to 375°. Prepare rigatoni according to package directions.
2. Meanwhile, spread oil on bottom of an 11- x 7-inch baking dish; add onion in a single layer.
3. Bake at 375° for 15 minutes or just until tender. Transfer onion to a large bowl, and set aside.
4. Drain chopped spinach well, pressing between layers of paper towels.
5. Stir rigatoni, spinach, chicken, and next 4 ingredients into onion in bowl. Spoon mixture into baking dish, and sprinkle evenly with shredded mozzarella cheese.
6. Bake, covered, at 375° for 30 minutes; uncover and bake 15 more minutes or until bubbly.

Simple Swap

For even more flavor, add an additional can of diced tomatoes.

Heavenly Chicken Lasagna

Makes 8 to 10 servings **Hands-on Time:** 15 min.

Total Time: 1 hr., 15 min.

1 Tbsp. butter or margarine
½ large onion, chopped
1 (10¾-oz.) can reduced-fat cream of chicken soup, undiluted
1 (10-oz.) container refrigerated reduced-fat Alfredo sauce
1 (7-oz.) jar sliced pimiento, undrained
1 (6-oz.) jar sliced mushrooms, drained
⅓ cup dry white wine
½ tsp. dried basil

1 (10-oz.) package frozen chopped spinach, thawed
1 cup cottage cheese
1 cup ricotta cheese
½ cup grated Parmesan cheese
1 large egg, lightly beaten
9 lasagna noodles, cooked
2½ cups chopped rotisserie chicken
3 cups (12 oz.) shredded sharp Cheddar cheese, divided

1. Preheat oven to 350°. Melt butter in a skillet over medium-high heat. Add onion, and sauté 5 minutes or until tender. Stir in soup and next 5 ingredients. Reserve 1 cup sauce.

2. Drain spinach well, pressing between layers of paper towels. Stir together spinach, cottage cheese, and next 3 ingredients.

3. Place 3 lasagna noodles in a lightly greased 13- x 9-inch baking dish. Layer with half each of sauce, spinach mixture, and chicken. Sprinkle with 1 cup Cheddar cheese. Repeat procedure. Top with remaining 3 noodles and reserved 1 cup sauce.

4. Bake at 350° for 45 minutes or until bubbly. Sprinkle with remaining 1 cup Cheddar cheese, and bake 5 more minutes or until cheese melts. Let stand 10 minutes before serving.

Grab and Go!

The quintessential Italian comfort food, this lasagna isn't complete without a fresh garden salad and toasted bread.

❏ *bagged salad*
❏ *1 bottle of your favorite dressing*
❏ *sliced bakery bread*

Chicken Vermicelli

Makes 6 to 8 servings **Hands-on Time:** 12 min. **Total Time:** 12 min.

1 (8.8-oz.) package
   vermicelli rice noodles
1 onion, diced
2 Tbsp. sesame oil
4 carrots, shredded
1 small head napa
   cabbage, finely chopped
3 medium celery ribs, diced
2 cups shredded rotisserie
   chicken

2 garlic cloves, minced
1 cup low-sodium fat-free
   chicken broth
1 Tbsp. cornstarch
¼ cup soy sauce
1 Tbsp. oyster sauce
Garnish: chopped green
   onions

1. Soak noodles in hot water 10 minutes; drain and set aside.
2. Meanwhile, sauté diced onion in hot oil in a large skillet over medium-high heat 5 minutes or until tender. Add carrots and next 4 ingredients; cook, stirring occasionally, 2 minutes or until vegetables are tender.
3. Stir together broth and cornstarch until smooth; add to chicken mixture. Add soy sauce and oyster sauce; bring mixture to a boil, and cook 1 minute. Remove from heat; serve over noodles. Garnish, if desired.

Simple Swap

This dish can also be made using spaghetti noodles. Simply cook according to package directions, and keep warm until adding the chicken mixture.

Grab and Go!

Ready in less than 15 minutes, this dish can be enjoyed on its own or paired with steam-in-bag snap peas.

❑ *steam-in-bag snap peas*

Lemon-Herb
Potatoes

ON THE SIDE

super simple sides to complete your chicken dinner

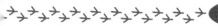
Green Beans with Tomatoes, Goat Cheese, and Almonds

Makes 6 to 8 servings **Hands-on Time:** 15 min. **Total Time:** 15 min.

2 lb. haricots verts (tiny green beans), trimmed
3 Tbsp. sherry vinegar*
2 Tbsp. fresh lemon juice
¾ tsp. salt
½ tsp. pepper
⅓ cup olive oil
1 pt. cherry tomatoes, halved

2 shallots, thinly sliced
2 garlic cloves, minced
½ (4-oz.) goat cheese log, crumbled
½ cup sliced almonds, toasted

1. Cook green beans in boiling salted water to cover 6 to 8 minutes or until crisp-tender; drain. Plunge beans into ice water to stop the cooking process; drain.
2. Meanwhile, whisk together vinegar and next 3 ingredients in a large bowl; add olive oil in a slow, steady stream, whisking constantly until blended and smooth. Add cherry tomatoes, shallots, garlic, and green beans; toss to coat.
3. Top green bean mixture with crumbled goat cheese and toasted almonds.

* White wine vinegar may be substituted.

FROM THE KITCHEN
To toast almonds, preheat oven to 350°. Bake almonds in a single layer in a shallow pan 6 to 8 minutes or until lightly toasted and fragrant, stirring halfway through.

Simple Swap

Green beans get a burst of flavor from tangy goat cheese. You can substitute feta cheese, if you prefer.

FROM THE KITCHEN

The lemon zest in this recipe gives the green beans a fresh-tasting flavor. You can substitute 1 Tbsp. lemon juice for the zest, if you prefer.

Rosemary Green Beans

Makes 6 servings **Hands-on Time:** 6 min. **Total Time:** 15 min.

1 lb. fresh green beans, trimmed
½ tsp. salt, divided
2 green onions, sliced (about ¼ cup)
2 tsp. chopped fresh rosemary
1 tsp. olive oil
¼ cup chopped pecans, toasted
2 tsp. lemon zest
Garnish: fresh rosemary sprigs

1. Sprinkle green beans evenly with ¼ tsp. salt, and place in a steamer basket over boiling water; cover and steam 10 minutes or until crisp-tender. Plunge green beans into ice water to stop the cooking process, and drain.

2. Sauté green onions and rosemary in hot oil in a nonstick skillet over medium-high heat 2 to 3 minutes or until softened. Add green beans, pecans, lemon zest, and remaining ¼ tsp. salt, stirring until thoroughly heated. Garnish, if desired, and serve immediately.

Simple Swap

If you don't have pecans but want to keep the crunch in this recipe, use toasted almonds instead.

Grilled Cheesy Corn

Makes 6 servings **Hands-on Time:** 10 min. **Total Time:** 30 min.

Chili powder gives intense flavor to plain corn in this recipe. Serving with fresh lime wedges adds a refreshing touch.

6 ears fresh corn
¼ cup melted butter
½ tsp. chili powder
½ tsp. smoked paprika
¼ tsp. salt
⅓ cup grated Cotija or Parmesan cheese
2 limes, cut into wedges

1. Preheat grill to 350° to 400° (medium-high) heat. Pull back husks from ears of fresh corn; remove and discard silks. Tie husks together with kitchen string to form a handle. Soak in cold salted water to cover 10 minutes; drain.

2. Grill corn, covered with grill lid, 15 minutes or until golden brown, turning occasionally. Remove from grill. Brush corn with melted butter; sprinkle with chili powder, smoked paprika, salt, and grated Cotija or Parmesan cheese. Serve with fresh lime wedges.

FROM THE KITCHEN

Chili powder, smoked paprika, and lime wedges give grilled corn a Southwestern touch. A brush with melted butter and cheese completes this dish.

Corn Pudding

Makes 6 servings **Hands-on Time:** 20 min. **Total Time:** 20 min.

2 cups milk
½ cup yellow cornmeal
  mix
1 (16-oz.) package frozen
  whole kernel corn,
  thawed
2 Tbsp. whipping cream
½ tsp. salt
Garnishes: chopped green
  onions, cooked and
  crumbled bacon

1. Bring milk to a boil in a heavy saucepan; gradually add cornmeal, stirring until blended after each addition. Cook, stirring constantly, just until mixture begins to boil. Reduce heat, and cook, stirring constantly, until thickened.
2. Add corn, stirring until mixture is consistency of whipped potatoes. Stir in whipping cream and salt. Garnish with chopped green onions and crumbled bacon, if desired.

FROM THE KITCHEN Be sure to add the cornmeal to the hot milk slowly and stir constantly with a wire whisk so that the pudding won't have lumps.

No need to wait for traditional corn pudding to bake in the oven—this version cooks up quickly on the stovetop!

Simple Swap

For an easy, on-hand alternative to cooked bacon, keep store-bought bacon bits in your fridge. You'll always have bacon crumbles ready to go.

A fast, vibrant side dish, asparagus gets an added touch of crunch from toasted almonds.

Oven-Roasted Asparagus

Makes 8 to 10 servings **Hands-on Time:** 5 min. **Total Time:** 15 min.

3 lb. fresh asparagus
2 Tbsp. olive oil
3 garlic cloves, minced
¾ tsp. salt

½ tsp. freshly ground
   pepper
½ cup slivered almonds,
   toasted

1. Preheat oven to 350°.
2. Snap off and discard tough ends of asparagus; place asparagus on a lightly greased baking sheet. Drizzle evenly with olive oil; sprinkle evenly with garlic, salt, and pepper.
3. Bake at 350° for 10 minutes or to desired degree of tenderness. Transfer asparagus to a serving dish; sprinkle with almonds.

FROM THE KITCHEN

To toast almonds, preheat oven to 350°. Bake almonds in a single layer in a shallow pan 6 to 8 minutes or until lightly toasted and fragrant, stirring halfway through.

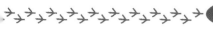

Sweet Corn and Zucchini

Makes 4 to 6 servings **Hands-on Time:** 12 min. **Total Time:** 12 min.

2 cups coarsely chopped zucchini	**2 cups fresh corn kernels (4 ears)**
½ cup diced sweet onion	**¼ cup chopped fresh chives**
3 Tbsp. butter	**2 tsp. taco seasoning mix**

1. Sauté zucchini and onion in butter in a large skillet over medium-high heat 5 minutes. Add corn kernels, chives, and taco seasoning mix; sauté 5 minutes or until tender.

Simple Swap

A welcome addition to any summer barbecue, this dish can also be made with frozen corn, if desired.

Take advantage of fresh vegetables from your local farmers' market for this smart side dish.

Avocado Fruit Salad

Makes 6 servings **Hands-on Time:** 8 min. **Total Time:** 1 hr., 8 min.

1 (24-oz.) jar refrigerated orange and grapefruit sections, rinsed, drained, and patted dry
1 (24-oz.) jar refrigerated tropical mixed fruit in light syrup, rinsed, drained, and patted dry
2 cups cubed fresh cantaloupe
1 medium-size ripe avocado, halved and cut into chunks
¼ cup chopped fresh mint
2 Tbsp. lime juice
Garnish: crushed pistachios

1. Toss together first 6 ingredients. Cover and chill 1 hour. Garnish, if desired.

Note: We tested with Del Monte SunFresh Citrus Salad and Del Monte SunFresh Tropical Mixed Fruit in Light Syrup with Passion Fruit Juice.

FROM THE KITCHEN

This dish can be prepared a day ahead; just don't cut the avocado or add the garnish until ready to serve.

Simple Swap

Make this recipe your own; try different fruit combinations to suit your taste.

Roasted Broccoli with Orange-Chipotle Butter

Makes 6 to 8 servings **Hands-on Time:** 6 min. **Total Time:** 21 min.

**2 (12-oz.) packages fresh
   broccoli florets**
2 Tbsp. olive oil
¼ cup butter, softened
2 tsp. orange zest

**1 tsp. minced canned
   chipotle pepper in
   adobo sauce**
½ tsp. salt

1. Preheat oven to 450°.

2. Combine broccoli and oil in a large bowl; toss to coat. Place broccoli in a single layer on an ungreased 15- x 10-inch jelly-roll pan. Roast at 450° for 15 to 17 minutes or until broccoli is crisp-tender.

3. While broccoli roasts, combine butter and next 3 ingredients in a large bowl. Add roasted broccoli to bowl, and toss to coat. Serve hot.

Simple Swap

You can also use one large head of broccoli in this recipe. Just break it apart, chop, and follow the recipe as directed.

FROM THE KITCHEN

Grate the orange zest over wax paper for easy cleanup. Gently run the fruit up and down a Microplane or the fine face of a box grater.

serve with

King Ranch
Chicken
Mac and Cheese

PAGE 191

Lemon Broccolini

Makes 6 to 8 servings **Hands-on Time:** 20 min. **Total Time:** 20 min.

1 cup (½-inch) French
   bread baguette cubes
2 Tbsp. butter
1 garlic clove, pressed
2 Tbsp. chopped fresh
   flat-leaf parsley

2 tsp. lemon zest
1½ lb. fresh Broccolini
2 Tbsp. fresh lemon juice
1 Tbsp. olive oil
Salt and freshly ground
   pepper to taste

1. Process bread in a food processor 30 seconds to 1 minute or until coarsely chopped.

2. Melt butter with garlic in a large skillet over medium heat; add breadcrumbs, and cook, stirring constantly, 2 to 3 minutes or until golden brown. Remove from heat, and stir in parsley and lemon zest.

3. Cook Broccolini in boiling salted water to cover 3 to 4 minutes or until crisp-tender; drain well. Toss Broccolini with lemon juice, olive oil, and salt and freshly ground pepper to taste. Transfer to a serving platter, and sprinkle with bread-crumb mixture.

FROM THE KITCHEN

This recipe is great for using up that leftover bread from the night before. Make sure to coarsely chop the bread cubes in a food processor before adding them to the garlic mixture.

Excellent with either frozen or fresh Brussels sprouts, this fancy fixin' only takes five ingredients to prepare.

Bacon-Brown Sugar Brussels Sprouts

Makes 6 to 8 servings **Hands-on Time:** 20 min. **Total Time:** 20 min.

4 bacon slices
1 (14-oz.) can chicken broth
1 Tbsp. brown sugar
1 tsp. salt
1½ lb. Brussels sprouts, trimmed and halved

1. Cook bacon in a Dutch oven over medium heat 10 minutes or until crisp. Remove bacon, and drain on paper towels, reserving drippings in Dutch oven. Crumble bacon.

2. Add broth, brown sugar, and salt to drippings in Dutch oven, and bring to a boil. Stir in Brussels sprouts. Cover and cook 6 to 8 minutes or until tender. Transfer Brussels sprouts to a serving bowl using a slotted spoon, and sprinkle with bacon. Serve immediately.

Simple Swap

If you are looking to switch things up, 4 oz. chopped pancetta would be a fantastic substitute for the bacon.

serve with
Chicken and Sweet Potato Pot Pie
PAGE 42

Orange-Curry Carrots

Makes 4 servings **Hands-on Time:** 5 min. **Total Time:** 10 min.

1 (1-lb.) package crinkle-cut carrots
⅓ cup orange marmalade
1 tsp. curry powder
½ tsp. salt
Freshly ground pepper (optional)

1. Place carrots and 3 Tbsp. water in a microwave-safe bowl. Cover bowl tightly with plastic wrap; fold back a small edge to allow steam to escape. Microwave at HIGH 5 minutes or until tender. Drain.

2. Stir together orange marmalade, curry powder, and salt. Toss gently with hot carrots. Sprinkle with pepper, if desired.

Simple Swap

Spicy and sweet, these curried carrots can be made with frozen or fresh crinkle-cuts. Just be sure to cook them thoroughly until tender before tossing them with the marmalade mixture.

Serve these kicked-up carrots next time you want a little sweet heat.

Simple Swap

Though this four-ingredient side dish is already simplicity at its best, you can also use bagged baby carrots for even quicker assembly.

Roasted Carrots

Makes 6 to 8 servings **Hands-on Time:** 5 min. **Total Time:** 40 min.

3 lb. small carrots with tops
1 Tbsp. olive oil
¾ tsp. salt
¼ tsp. freshly ground
pepper

1. Preheat oven to 450°. Peel carrots, if desired. Trim tops to 1 inch.

2. Toss carrots with oil, salt, and pepper. Place on a 15- x 10-inch jelly-roll pan.

3. Bake at 450° for 20 minutes, stirring once. Reduce heat to 325°, and bake, stirring occasionally, 15 more minutes or until carrots are browned and tender.

FROM THE KITCHEN If you have thick carrots, cut them lengthwise so that they cook evenly.

 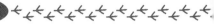
Simple Swap

Delicious and nutritious, fresh or frozen cauliflower works great in this recipe. You can also add broccoli florets for a burst of color.

Curried Cauliflower

Makes 4 servings **Hands-on Time:** 5 min. **Total Time:** 13 min.

1 tsp. curry powder	**2 (10-oz.) packages fresh**
¼ tsp. dried crushed red	**cauliflower florets**
pepper	**1 medium onion, chopped**
2 Tbsp. vegetable oil	**¾ tsp. salt**

1. Cook curry powder and red pepper in hot oil in a large skillet over medium heat, stirring often, 1 minute. Add cauliflower, onion, and salt, and cook, stirring constantly, 2 to 3 minutes or until onion is crisp-tender. Reduce heat to low; add 6 Tbsp. water.

2. Cover and cook, stirring occasionally, 8 to 10 minutes or just until cauliflower is tender.

serve with
**Spicy Chicken-
Rice Bowl**
PAGE 211

Brown Butter-Cauliflower Mash

Makes 6 servings **Hands-on Time:** 10 min. **Total Time:** 20 min.

2 (16-oz.) packages frozen
   cauliflower
½ cup sour cream
¾ tsp. salt
½ tsp. pepper
¼ cup grated Parmesan
   cheese

1 Tbsp. chopped fresh
   chives
2 Tbsp. butter
Garnish: fresh chives

1. Cook cauliflower according to package directions. Process cauliflower, sour cream, salt, and pepper in a food processor 30 seconds to 1 minute or until smooth, stopping to scrape down sides as needed. Stir in Parmesan cheese and chives. Place in a bowl.

2. If desired, microwave mixture at HIGH 1 to 2 minutes or until thoroughly heated, stirring at 1-minute intervals.

3. Cook butter in a small heavy saucepan over medium heat, stirring constantly, 4 to 5 minutes or until butter begins to turn golden brown. Remove from heat, and immediately drizzle butter over cauliflower mixture. Garnish, if desired. Serve immediately.

Simple Swap

You can also use bagged, fresh cauliflower florets in this recipe. Just steam according to directions.

FROM THE KITCHEN

Brown butter gives the cauliflower a rich, nutty flavor in this recipe.

Blue Cheese and Green Onion Potato Salad

Makes 8 servings **Hands-on Time:** 10 min. **Total Time:** 20 min.

3 lb. new potatoes, quartered
2 tsp. salt, divided
⅓ cup sliced green onions
1 (8-oz.) container sour cream
½ cup bottled refrigerated blue cheese dressing
½ tsp. freshly ground pepper
½ cup crumbled blue cheese

1. Bring potatoes, 1 tsp. salt, and water to cover to a boil. Cook 10 to 15 minutes or just until tender; drain.

2. Stir together green onions, next 3 ingredients, and remaining 1 tsp. salt in a large bowl; add potatoes and crumbled blue cheese, stirring gently to coat. Serve immediately, or cover and chill until ready to serve.

Simple Swap

For an extra flavor boost, add crumbled, cooked bacon to this hearty side.

Lemon-Herb Potatoes

Makes 8 to 10 servings **Hands-on Time:** 5 min. **Total Time:** 20 min.

3 lb. baby red potatoes, halved
¾ cup assorted chopped fresh herbs
¼ cup olive oil
3 Tbsp. fresh lemon juice
1 garlic clove, minced

1. Bring potatoes and salted water to cover to a boil in a large saucepan. Cook 10 to 15 minutes or until tender; drain. Toss potatoes with chopped fresh herbs, olive oil, fresh lemon juice, and minced garlic.

Simple Swap

For fantastic flavor, try a variety of your favorite herbs, such as rosemary, chives, parsley, and thyme, in this recipe.

This zesty dish is sure to be a hit at your next barbecue or as a simple weeknight side. It can be enjoyed warm, chilled, or at room temperature.

Spring Potato Toss

Makes 8 to 10 servings **Hands-on Time:** 5 min. **Total Time:** 20 min.

3 lb. baby red potatoes, quartered

1½ cups frozen sweet peas, thawed

½ cup jarred refrigerated pesto sauce

2 Tbsp. lemon juice

¼ cup cooked and crumbled bacon

1. Bring potatoes and salted water to cover to a boil in a large saucepan. Cook 10 to 15 minutes or until tender; drain.

2. Gently toss potatoes with peas, pesto, and lemon juice. Sprinkle with bacon.

FROM THE KITCHEN

The heat from the just-boiled potatoes is enough to warm the thawed peas that add a punch of bright color and flavor to this side.

serve with
**Snappy Smoth-
ered Chicken**
page 206

Perfect Mashed Potatoes

Makes 10 to 12 servings **Hands-on Time:** 18 min.
Total Time: 45 min.

3 lb. Yukon gold potatoes
2 tsp. salt, divided
⅓ cup butter
⅓ cup half-and-half

4 oz. cream cheese, softened
¾ tsp. coarsely ground pepper

1. Peel potatoes, and cut into 1-inch pieces. Bring potatoes, 1 tsp. salt, and cold water to cover to a boil in a medium-size Dutch oven over medium-high heat. Reduce heat to medium-low, and cook 16 to 20 minutes or until fork-tender; drain.

2. Return potatoes to Dutch oven. Cook until water evaporates and potatoes look dry. Mound potatoes on 1 side; add butter, next 3 ingredients, and remaining 1 tsp. salt to opposite side of Dutch oven. Cook 1 to 2 minutes or until butter melts and mixture boils.

3. Remove from heat; beat at medium speed with a hand-held electric mixer 30 seconds to 1 minute or to desired degree of smoothness. (Do not overbeat.) Serve immediately.

Simple Swap

To add a little extra flavor to this side, try substituting chive-and-onion cream cheese for the plain cream cheese.

Yukon gold potatoes yield a texture that's just right for serving with flavorful gravy or melted butter.

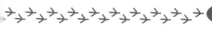 
From-Scratch Oven Fries

Makes 4 servings **Hands-on Time:** 10 min. **Total Time:** 50 min.

1½ lb. medium-size baking potatoes, peeled and cut into ½-inch-thick strips

1 Tbsp. vegetable oil
½ tsp. kosher or table salt
Ketchup (optional)

1. Preheat oven to 450°. Rinse potatoes in cold water. Drain and pat dry. Toss together potatoes, oil, and salt in a large bowl.
2. Place a lightly greased wire rack in a 15- x 10-inch jelly-roll pan. Arrange potatoes in a single layer on wire rack.
3. Bake at 450° for 40 to 45 minutes or until browned, turning halfway through. Serve immediately with ketchup, if desired.

Italian-Parmesan Oven Fries: Toss 2 tsp. freshly ground Italian seasoning with potato mixture, and bake as directed. Sprinkle warm fries with 2 Tbsp. grated Parmesan cheese. Serve with warmed jarred marinara sauce, if desired.

FROM THE KITCHEN

These homemade kid-favorite fries are best enjoyed right from the oven. For fries with a kick of spice, add a pinch of ground red pepper before cooking.

Serving this dish with orange and lemon slices lets you use every bit of the orange and lemon needed for the zest.

Citrus-Scented Rice with Fresh Basil

Makes 4 servings **Hands-on Time:** 5 min. **Total Time:** 25 min.

2 cups chicken broth
2 Tbsp. butter
1 Tbsp. orange zest
2 Tbsp. fresh orange juice
1 tsp. lemon zest
1 cup uncooked basmati rice

3 Tbsp. chopped fresh basil
Garnishes: orange and
   lemon slices, orange
   zest, lemon zest

1. Stir together chicken broth, butter, orange zest, fresh orange juice, and lemon zest in a large saucepan; bring to a boil over high heat.

2. Stir in basmati rice; cover, reduce heat to low, and cook 20 minutes or until liquid is absorbed and rice is tender. Stir in basil. Garnish, if desired.

Simple Swap

If you don't have fresh basil on hand, try using ½ tsp. dried basil to achieve the full flavor of this dish; just add it to the broth in the first step.

Cheddar Drop Biscuits

Makes 12 biscuits **Hands-on Time:** 6 min. **Total Time:** 14 min.

2 cups all-purpose
    baking mix
½ cup (2 oz.) shredded
    sharp Cheddar cheese
¾ cup milk

Vegetable cooking spray
2 Tbsp. butter, melted
½ tsp. dried parsley,
    crushed
½ tsp. garlic powder

1. Preheat oven to 450°. Combine baking mix and cheese; make a well in center of mixture. Add milk, stirring just until moistened.

2. Drop dough by rounded tablespoonfuls, 2 inches apart, onto a baking sheet coated with cooking spray. Bake at 450° for 8 minutes or until golden.

3. Combine butter, parsley, and garlic powder; brush over warm biscuits.

FROM THE KITCHEN

Due to a higher proportion of liquid to the dry ingredients, drop biscuits have a thinner batter than a soft dough such as rolled biscuits, which is why they're dropped instead of kneaded and rolled.

These restaurant-style buttery biscuits won't last long. However, you can save leftovers in an airtight container for up to two days; just reheat a few seconds in the microwave when you are ready to enjoy them.

Three-Seed Pan Rolls

Makes 9 rolls **Hands-on Time:** 10 min. **Total Time:** 3 hr., 25 min.

FROM THE KITCHEN

You can omit the fennel seeds in this recipe and still impress with this scrumptious side bread.

4 tsp. fennel seeds
4 tsp. poppy seeds
4 tsp. sesame seeds

9 frozen bread dough rolls
1 egg white, beaten
2 Tbsp. butter, melted

1. Combine first 3 ingredients in a small bowl. Dip rolls, 1 at a time, in egg white; roll in seed mixture. Arrange rolls, 1 inch apart, in a lightly greased 8-inch pan. Cover with lightly greased plastic wrap, and let rise in a warm place (85°), free from drafts, 3 to 4 hours or until doubled in bulk.

2. Preheat oven to 350°. Uncover rolls, and bake at 350° for 15 minutes or until golden. Brush with melted butter.

Note: We tested with Rhodes White Dinner Rolls.

Three-Seed French Bread: Substitute 1 (11-oz.) can refrigerated French bread dough for frozen bread dough rolls. Combine seeds in a shallow dish. Brush dough loaf with egg white. Roll top and sides of dough loaf in seeds. Place, seam side down, on a baking sheet. Cut slits across top of dough and bake dough loaf according to package directions.

These rolls may look like cinnamon rolls, but they are packed with savory rosemary and briny olives! They're great alongside a warmed rotisserie chicken.

Simple Swap

Asiago has a sweeter flavor than Parmesan and Romano, but either of these hard cheeses would be a great substitute.

Easy Asiago-Olive Rolls

Makes 10 rolls **Hands-on Time:** 10 min. **Total Time:** 25 min.

1 (13.8-oz.) can refrigerated pizza crust dough
¼ cup refrigerated olive tapenade
½ cup grated Asiago cheese
1 tsp. chopped fresh rosemary
1 Tbsp. butter, melted

1. Preheat oven to 450°.

2. Unroll pizza crust dough. Spread olive tapenade over dough, leaving a ¼-inch border. Sprinkle with cheese and rosemary. Gently roll up dough, starting at 1 long side. Cut into 10 (1¼-inch-thick) slices.

3. Place slices in a lightly greased 9-inch round cake pan. Brush top of dough with melted butter. Bake at 450° for 15 to 20 minutes or until golden. Serve immediately.

FROM THE KITCHEN
Bake up a double batch of these effortlessly excellent rolls. You can freeze the extras for later.

serve with
White Lightning
Chicken Chili
page 71

Sour Cream Cornsticks

Makes 16 cornsticks **Hands-on Time:** 5 min. **Total Time:** 21 min.

3 large eggs, lightly beaten
1 cup self-rising
    cornmeal mix
1 (8¾-oz.) can cream-style
    corn

1 (8-oz.) container sour
    cream
¼ cup vegetable oil

1. Preheat oven to 400°. Heat 2 lightly greased cast-iron cornstick pans in oven 5 minutes.
2. Combine all ingredients, stirring just until cornmeal is moistened.
3. Remove cast-iron pans from oven, and spoon batter into hot pans.
4. Bake at 400° for 16 to 18 minutes or until golden. Remove from pans and serve immediately.

> **FROM THE KITCHEN**
> Self-rising cornmeal mix has all the leavening and salt added, so it minimizes prep time by reducing the number of ingredients needed.

Cooking cornbread in these corn cob-shaped pans is not only great for presentation, but it also results in individual pieces for the whole family.

Broccoli-Cornbread Muffins

Makes 36 mini muffins **Hands-on Time:** 10 min. **Total Time:** 27 min.

1 (8½-oz.) package corn muffin mix
1 (10-oz.) package frozen chopped broccoli, thawed and drained
1 cup (4 oz.) shredded Cheddar cheese
1 small onion, chopped
2 large eggs
½ cup butter, melted

1. Preheat oven to 325°. Combine first 4 ingredients in a large bowl; make a well in center of mixture.

2. Stir together eggs and butter, blending well; add to broccoli mixture, stirring just until dry ingredients are moistened. Spoon into 2 lightly greased (24-cup) miniature muffin pans, filling three-fourths full.

3. Bake at 325° for 15 to 20 minutes or until golden. Let stand 2 to 3 minutes before removing from pans.

FROM THE KITCHEN

You can also make these muffins in regular-size (12-cup) pans; bake 20 to 24 minutes or until golden.

You can enjoy these mini muffins with breakfast, lunch, or dinner.

King Ranch Chicken
Mac and Cheese

TAKE IT WITH YOU

portable feasts for picnics, potlucks, and family gatherings

Assemble this salad right before serving so that the greens stay crisp.

Layered Chicken Cobb Salad

Makes 10 to 12 servings **Hands-on Time:** 30 min.
Total Time: 30 min.

1 ripe avocado
1 cup refrigerated Ranch dressing
8 cups shredded romaine lettuce
4 cups chopped rotisserie chicken
1 cup fresh corn kernels (2 ears)

8 hard-cooked eggs, peeled and chopped
1½ cups chopped tomato
8 cooked bacon slices, crumbled
1 cup crumbled blue cheese

1. Cut avocado in half. Scoop avocado pulp into bowl; mash with a fork or potato masher until smooth. Stir in dressing.
2. Layer half each of lettuce, chicken, corn, egg, tomato, bacon, and cheese in a 4-qt. trifle bowl or straight-sided clear bowl. Drizzle with half of dressing mixture. Repeat layers once, ending with dressing mixture.

FROM THE KITCHEN

To transport this salad to a party, keep prepped salad ingredients in zip-top plastic freezer bags, and assemble the salad in a large bowl or in individual servings. Drizzle all the dressing on top, or serve the dressing on the side.

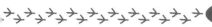
Chicken-and-Broccoli Salad

Makes 6 servings **Hands-on Time:** 10 min. **Total Time:** 10 min.

1 cup mayonnaise
3 Tbsp. sugar
2 Tbsp. cider vinegar
4 cups chopped rotisserie chicken
2 cups finely chopped fresh broccoli
½ cup diced red onion
½ cup sweetened dried cranberries
½ cup toasted chopped pecans
¼ tsp. salt
¼ tsp. freshly ground pepper
⅓ cup cooked and crumbled bacon

1. Whisk together mayonnaise, sugar, and vinegar in a large bowl. Stir in chicken and next 6 ingredients. Sprinkle with bacon just before serving.

FROM THE KITCHEN
Ready in minutes, this easy chicken salad recipe is great for summer picnics or potlucks. Wait to add the bacon until just before you are ready to serve so that it stays crispy.

From chopped broccoli to crumbled bacon, this bold, standout chicken salad is packed with lots of crunch!

Simple Swap

If you don't have dried cranberries on hand, try raisins for a sweet substitution.

Store-bought pesto makes this dish superfast! With a sprinkle of pine nuts and feta, this hearty potato chicken salad is a crowd-pleaser.

Pesto Chicken Potato Salad

Makes 4 to 6 servings **Hands-on Time:** 16 min.
Total Time: 1 hr., 32 min.

1½ lb. red potatoes, cut
   into 1-inch pieces
½ cup jarred pesto sauce
½ tsp. lemon zest
2 cups shredded rotisserie
   chicken

¼ cup pine nuts, toasted
2 oz. crumbled feta cheese
Garnish: basil leaves

1. Bring potatoes and water to cover to a boil in a large saucepan over medium-high heat, and cook 15 minutes or until tender. Drain. Cool slightly.

2. Stir together pesto and lemon zest in a large bowl. Add potatoes and chicken, and toss until well blended. Sprinkle with pine nuts and feta cheese. Cover and chill at least 1 hour. Garnish, if desired.

FROM THE KITCHEN

Make this potato salad a day ahead. Place in an airtight storage container, and it's ready to go when you are.

Bacon-Chicken Salad

Makes 3⅓ cups **Hands-on Time:** 13 min. **Total Time:** 13 min.

Take this flavorful salad to your next picnic, and serve it with crackers, or make sandwiches using sliced sourdough bread, lettuce leaves, and tomato slices.

¾ cup mayonnaise
1 Tbsp. chopped fresh chives
2 tsp. lemon juice
½ tsp. salt
½ tsp. freshly ground pepper

3 cups shredded rotisserie chicken
6 cooked bacon slices, crumbled
½ cup chopped toasted pecans

1. Stir together first 5 ingredients in a large bowl. Fold in chicken, bacon, and pecans. Serve immediately, or cover and chill.

Time-Saver

This is a great recipe to use up leftover bacon from breakfast—just crumble it, and stir in.

BBQ Chicken Casserole with Cornbread Crust

Makes 6 servings **Hands-on Time:** 21 min. **Total Time:** 56 min.

1 cup chopped red onion
1 Tbsp. canola oil
4 cups shredded rotisserie chicken
1 cup bottled spicy barbecue sauce
½ cup chopped green onions, divided

1 (8½-oz.) package corn muffin mix
⅓ cup milk
1 large egg
½ cup (2 oz.) shredded sharp Cheddar cheese
½ cup (2 oz.) shredded white Cheddar cheese

1. Preheat oven to 350°. Sauté onion in hot oil in a small skillet over medium-high heat 5 minutes or until tender. Transfer onion to a large bowl. Stir in chicken, barbecue sauce, and ¼ cup green onions. Spoon mixture into a lightly greased 11- x 7-inch baking dish.

2. Stir together corn muffin mix, milk, and egg in a medium bowl. Fold remaining ¼ cup green onions and ¼ cup of each cheese into batter. Spread cornbread batter evenly over chicken mixture. Sprinkle remaining ¼ cup of each cheese over batter.

3. Bake at 350° for 35 minutes or until crust is golden.

The spicy barbecue sauce offsets the sweet flavor of the cornbread topping.

Simple Swap

Use your favorite cornbread mix and barbecue sauce to create your own combination of flavors.

Salsa Verde Chicken Casserole

Makes 8 servings **Hands-on Time:** 15 min. **Total Time:** 45 min.

2 (3.5-oz.) bags boil-in-bag rice
2 ripe avocados
¾ cup salsa verde
1 (4.5-oz.) can chopped green chiles, drained
1 Tbsp. fresh lime juice
2 cups chopped rotisserie chicken breast

1 (10¾-oz.) can reduced-fat cream of chicken soup
1 cup light sour cream
1 cup (4 oz.) shredded Monterey Jack cheese
2 Tbsp. chopped fresh cilantro
Topping: chopped tomatoes

1. Preheat oven to 350°. Prepare rice according to package directions.
2. Meanwhile, cut avocados in half. Scoop avocado pulp into a medium bowl, and mash with salsa verde, chopped green chiles, and lime juice. Stir in hot cooked rice.
3. Stir together chicken, soup, and sour cream in a small saucepan over low heat; cook, stirring occasionally, 5 minutes or until blended and slightly heated.
4. Spoon rice mixture into a lightly greased 13- x 9-inch baking dish; spoon chicken mixture over rice. Sprinkle with Monterey Jack cheese.
5. Bake at 350° for 30 minutes or until cheese melts and casserole is bubbly. Sprinkle with chopped cilantro. Top with chopped tomatoes.

Grab and Go!

For an easy, effortless side, pair this recipe with some refried beans.

❑ *can of refried beans*

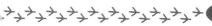
Chicken Tetrazzini

Makes 12 servings **Hands-on Time:** 20 min. **Total Time:** 55 min.

1 (16-oz.) package
   vermicelli
½ cup chicken broth
4 cups chopped rotisserie
   chicken
1 (10¾-oz.) can cream of
   mushroom soup
1 (10¾-oz.) can cream of
   chicken soup
1 (10¾-oz.) can cream of
   celery soup

1 (8-oz.) container sour
   cream
1 (6-oz.) jar sliced
   mushrooms, drained
½ cup (2 oz.) shredded
   Parmesan cheese
1 tsp. freshly ground
   pepper
½ tsp. salt
2 cups (8 oz.) shredded
   Cheddar cheese

1. Preheat oven to 350°. Cook vermicelli according to package directions; drain. Return to pot, and toss with chicken broth.

2. Meanwhile, stir together chicken and next 8 ingredients in a large bowl; add vermicelli, and toss well. Spoon chicken mixture into 2 lightly greased 11- x 7-inch baking dishes. Sprinkle with Cheddar cheese.

3. Bake, covered, at 350° for 30 minutes. Uncover and bake 5 more minutes or until cheese is bubbly.

Simple Swap

Make the most out of on-hand ingredients. Use regular spaghetti noodles in place of vermicelli, if desired.

Vermicelli is a thin spaghetti-like pasta that is perfect in this casserole to soak up all the creamy sauce.

FROM THE KITCHEN

To make ahead, freeze unbaked casserole up to 1 month. Thaw casserole overnight in refrigerator. Let stand 30 minutes at room temperature, and bake as directed.

King Ranch Chicken Mac and Cheese

Makes 6 servings **Hands-on Time:** 15 min. **Total Time:** 40 min.

1 (8-oz.) package cellentani pasta
2 Tbsp. butter
1 medium onion, diced
1 green bell pepper, diced
1 (10-oz.) can diced tomatoes and green chiles
1 (8-oz.) package pasteurized prepared cheese product, cubed
3 cups chopped rotisserie chicken
1 (10¾-oz.) can cream of chicken soup
½ cup sour cream
1 tsp. chili powder
½ tsp. ground cumin
1½ cups (6 oz.) shredded Cheddar cheese

1. Preheat oven to 350°. Prepare pasta according to package directions.

2. Meanwhile, melt butter in a large Dutch oven over medium-high heat. Add onion and bell pepper, and sauté 5 minutes or until tender. Stir in tomatoes and green chiles and prepared cheese product; cook, stirring constantly, 2 minutes or until cheese melts. Stir in chicken, next 4 ingredients, and hot cooked pasta until blended. Spoon mixture into a lightly greased 10-inch cast-iron skillet or 11- x 7-inch baking dish; sprinkle with shredded Cheddar cheese.

3. Bake at 350° for 25 to 30 minutes or until bubbly.

Two comfort food all-stars come together in a dish your family will ask for again and again.

Time-Saver

Double this recipe, freeze it after Step 2, and use it when you need dinner fast! Just thaw the casserole in the fridge overnight, let it rest at room temperature 30 minutes, and bake according to directions.

Grab and Go!

To complete this rich and creamy recipe, serve it alongside steamed broccoli or green beans.

❑ 1 bag steam-in-bag broccoli florets or green beans

Buttery cracker topping is the special touch in this casserole. Don't forget to add the crushed crackers just before baking.

Cheesy Chicken Casserole

Makes 4 to 6 servings **Hands-on Time:** 15 min. **Total Time:** 50 min.

3 cups shredded rotisserie chicken

1 (10¾-oz.) can cream of chicken and mushroom soup

1 (8-oz.) container sour cream

¼ tsp. freshly ground pepper

1 (8-oz.) package shredded sharp Cheddar cheese, divided

25 round buttery crackers, coarsely crushed

1. Preheat oven to 350°. Stir together chicken, soup, sour cream, pepper, and 1½ cups cheese; spoon mixture into a lightly greased 2-qt. baking dish.

2. Combine remaining ½ cup cheese and cracker crumbs; sprinkle evenly over top.

3. Bake casserole at 350° for 30 minutes or until bubbly. Let stand 5 minutes before serving.

FROM THE KITCHEN

To make ahead, prepare the recipe through Step 1, cover, and chill overnight. Uncover and continue with instructions the next day.

Chicken-and-Rice Casserole

Makes 8 servings **Hands-on Time:** 20 min. **Total Time:** 40 min.

2 Tbsp. butter
1 medium onion, chopped
1 (8.8-oz.) pouch ready-to-serve rice
3 cups chopped rotisserie chicken
1½ cups frozen petite peas
1½ cups (6 oz.) shredded sharp Cheddar cheese

1 cup mayonnaise
1 (10¾-oz.) can cream of chicken soup
1 (8-oz.) can sliced water chestnuts, drained
1 (4-oz.) jar sliced pimientos, drained
3 cups coarsely crushed ridged potato chips

1. Preheat oven to 350°. Melt butter in a skillet over medium heat. Add onion, and sauté 5 minutes or until tender.

2. Cook rice in microwave according to package directions. Combine sautéed onion, rice, chicken, and next 6 ingredients in a large bowl; toss gently. Spoon mixture into a lightly greased 13- x 9-inch baking dish. Top with coarsely crushed potato chips.

3. Bake, uncovered, at 350° for 20 to 25 minutes or until bubbly.

Crushed chips are a retro but surefire way to add crunch and extra flavor to this homestyle casserole.

FROM THE KITCHEN

To make ahead, prepare and spoon the casserole into a baking dish, leaving off the crushed chips. Cover and chill up to 24 hours. Uncover and add crushed chips before baking.

A pan of hot lasagna is a great way to welcome new neighbors or comfort a sick friend.

Simple Swap

For a lighter lasagna, substitute reduced-fat Alfredo sauce and reduced-fat cream of mushroom soup.

Chicken-and-Spinach Lasagna

Makes 6 servings **Hands-on Time:** 20 min.
Total Time: 4 hr., 30 min.

1 (10-oz.) package frozen chopped spinach, thawed
3 cups chopped rotisserie chicken
2 cups matchstick carrots
2 (10-oz.) packages refrigerated Alfredo sauce

1 (10¾-oz.) can cream of mushroom soup
1 cup chicken broth
½ tsp. pepper
4 cups (16 oz.) shredded Italian cheese blend, divided
9 uncooked lasagna noodles

1. Drain spinach well, pressing between paper towels. Stir together spinach, chicken, next 5 ingredients, and 3 cups Italian cheese blend in a large bowl.

2. Spoon one-fourth of chicken mixture into a lightly greased 6-qt. slow cooker. Arrange 3 noodles over chicken mixture, breaking to fit. Repeat layers twice. Top with remaining chicken mixture and 1 cup cheese.

3. Cover and cook on LOW 3½ hours or until noodles are done, mixture is bubbly, and edges are golden brown. Uncover and cook on LOW 30 more minutes. Let stand 10 minutes before serving.

Chicken-and-Sausage
Jambalaya

WEEKNIGHT COMPANY

fancy feasts that impress with little effort

Chicken-and-Potato Pancakes

Makes 6 to 8 servings **Hands-on Time:** 15 min. **Total Time:** 24 min.

2 cups instant pancake mix
2 cups milk
2 cups shredded rotisserie chicken
1½ cups (6 oz.) shredded Colby-Jack cheese blend
1 cup refrigerated shredded hash browns
4 green onions, finely chopped
2 Tbps. butter, melted
½ tsp. salt
¼ tsp. pepper
Quick Cream Gravy (optional)

1. Whisk together pancake mix and milk in a large bowl, whisking just until dry ingredients are moistened. Stir in chicken and next 6 ingredients, stirring just until blended.
2. Pour about ¼ cup batter for each cake onto a hot, lightly greased griddle or large nonstick skillet. Cook pancakes 3 minutes or until tops are covered with bubbles and edges look dry and cooked; turn and cook other side 5 to 6 minutes or until done. Serve with Quick Cream Gravy, if desired.

Note: We tested with Aunt Jemima Complete Pancake & Waffle Mix and Simply Potatoes Shredded Hash Browns.

Quick Cream Gravy

Bring ¼ cup **dry white wine** to a boil over medium heat in a small saucepan. Reduce heat to medium-low, and cook 1 minute. Add 1 cup **water;** whisk in 1 (1.2-oz.) package **roasted chicken gravy mix** and ¼ tsp. **pepper.** Increase heat to medium, and return to a boil. Reduce heat to low, and simmer 3 minutes or until thickened. Whisk in 2 Tbsp. **heavy cream.** Makes 1¼ cups.

Note: We tested with Knorr Roasted Chicken Gravy Mix.

FROM THE KITCHEN

The secret to tender pancakes? Mix the batter just long enough to incorporate the ingredients, and flip them only once.

Simple Swap

To make **Chicken-and-Rice Cakes,** substitute shredded **Italian three-cheese blend** for Colby-Jack cheese blend **and 1 cup cooked rice for** hash browns. Proceed with recipe as directed.

Creamy Chicken-and-Polenta Casserole

Makes 8 servings **Hands-on Time:** 15 min. **Total Time:** 50 min.

1 (32-oz.) container chicken broth
2 Tbsp. butter or margarine
½ tsp. freshly ground pepper
1 cup plain yellow cornmeal
¾ cup (3 oz.) shredded Parmesan cheese
1 (12-oz.) jar marinated quartered artichoke hearts, drained and coarsely chopped
1 (12-oz.) jar roasted red bell peppers, drained and chopped
4 cups shredded rotisserie chicken
1 (15-oz.) jar roasted garlic Alfredo sauce
⅓ cup chopped fresh basil
1½ cups (6 oz.) shredded Italian three-cheese blend

1. Bring first 3 ingredients to a boil in a large saucepan; gradually whisk in cornmeal. Cook 4 minutes or until thickened and bubbly, stirring constantly. Remove from heat; stir in Parmesan cheese. Spoon polenta evenly into 2 (8-inch) square pans. Cool 10 minutes.

2. Sprinkle artichoke hearts, peppers, and chicken evenly over polenta. Pour Alfredo sauce over chicken in both pans. Sprinkle with basil; top with Italian cheese blend. Cover and chill until ready to bake.

3. Bake, uncovered, at 350° for 25 minutes or until casserole is thoroughly heated.

Note: We tested with Classico Alfredo Sauce.

Grab and Go!

For an easy addition to this Mediterranean meal, serve with rustic bread from the bakery section of the store.

❑ *1 loaf of bakery bread*

Stovetop Chicken Pie

Makes 6 to 8 servings **Hands-on Time:** 22 min. **Total Time:** 22 min.

8 frozen buttermilk biscuits
1 small sweet onion, diced
1 Tbsp. canola oil
1 (8-oz.) package sliced
 fresh mushrooms
4 cups sliced rotisserie
 chicken
1 (10¾-oz.) can reduced-fat
 cream of mushroom soup
1 cup low-sodium fat-free
 chicken broth

½ cup dry white wine
½ (8-oz.) package ⅓-less-fat
 cream cheese, cubed
½ (0.7-oz.) envelope Italian
 dressing mix (about
 2 tsp.)
1 cup frozen baby peas,
 thawed

1. Bake biscuits according to package directions.
2. Meanwhile, sauté onion in hot oil in a large skillet over medium-high heat 5 minutes or until golden. Add mushrooms, and sauté 5 minutes or until tender. Stir in chicken and next 5 ingredients; cook, stirring frequently, 5 minutes or until cheese is melted and mixture is thoroughly heated. Stir in peas, and cook 2 minutes. Spoon chicken mixture over hot split biscuits.

FROM THE KITCHEN
Any kind of biscuits will work in this recipe—canned, frozen, or from scratch.

Simple Swap

While hot biscuits are the classic base, you can also spoon the chicken mixture over rice for a satisfying swap.

Smothered Chicken is a beloved Southern classic. This speedy version uses a rotisserie chicken cut into breast, wing, leg, and thigh pieces.

Simple Swap

We added a little white wine to this recipe to dress it up a bit. If you prefer not to use wine, increase the milk to 1⅓ cups.

Snappy Smothered Chicken

Makes 4 servings **Hands-on Time:** 18 min. **Total Time:** 28 min.

1 (8-oz.) package wide egg noodles
1 tsp. paprika
1 tsp. dried thyme leaves, crumbled
½ tsp. salt
¼ tsp. pepper
3 Tbsp. butter
1 large onion, chopped
2 (8-oz.) packages sliced fresh mushrooms

2 tsp. jarred minced garlic
1 (10¾-oz.) can cream of mushroom soup
1 cup milk
⅓ cup dry white wine
1 rotisserie chicken, cut into serving pieces
2 Tbsp. chopped fresh parsley

1. Prepare noodles according to package directions. Keep warm.
2. Meanwhile, stir together paprika, dried thyme, salt, and pepper in a small bowl.
3. Melt butter in a large skillet over medium-high heat; add onion and mushrooms, and sauté 8 to 10 minutes or until onion is tender. Stir in garlic and paprika mixture; sauté 2 minutes. Add soup, milk, and wine, and bring to a boil, stirring frequently. Add chicken pieces; spoon sauce over top of chicken. Reduce heat to low, and cook, covered, 10 to 15 minutes or until chicken is thoroughly heated. Stir in 1 Tbsp. parsley. Serve over hot cooked noodles. Sprinkle with remaining parsley.

Chicken-and-Black Bean Enchiladas

Makes 4 to 6 servings **Hands-on Time:** 10 min. **Total Time:** 45 min.

3 cups shredded rotisserie chicken
1 (15-oz.) can black beans, drained and rinsed
1 (10-oz.) can diced tomatoes with green chiles, undrained
1 (8¾-oz.) can no-salt-added corn, drained
1 (8-oz.) package shredded reduced-fat Mexican four-cheese blend, divided
8 (8-inch) whole wheat flour tortillas
Vegetable cooking spray
2 (10-oz.) cans enchilada sauce

1. Preheat oven to 350°.
2. Combine first 4 ingredients and 1½ cups cheese in a large bowl. Spoon chicken mixture evenly down the center of each tortilla, and roll up. Arrange, seam side down, in a 13- x 9-inch baking dish coated with cooking spray.
3. Pour enchilada sauce evenly over tortillas, and sprinkle evenly with remaining ½ cup cheese.
4. Bake, covered, at 350° for 20 minutes. Remove foil, and bake 15 more minutes or until bubbly.

Grab and Go!

Serve this saucy main with a side of Spanish rice.

❏ *1 (8.8-oz) pouch ready-to-serve spanish-style rice*

Spicy Chicken-Rice Bowl

Makes 6 servings **Hands-on Time:** 15 min. **Total Time:** 15 min.

1½ cups uncooked long-
   grain rice
2 Tbsp. butter
1 Tbsp. all-purpose flour
1¼ cups chicken broth
½ cup milk
½ cup light coconut milk
3 Tbsp. red curry paste
2 Tbsp. fresh lime juice
2 tsp. grated fresh ginger
½ tsp. salt

3 cups shredded rotisserie
   chicken
1½ cups fresh steamed
   green beans, cut into
   1-inch pieces
½ red bell pepper, cut into
   thin strips
¼ cup chopped fresh
   cilantro
Lime wedges

1. Prepare rice according to package directions.

2. Meanwhile, melt butter in a heavy saucepan over low heat; whisk in flour until smooth. Cook, whisking constantly, 1 minute. Gradually whisk in chicken broth, milk, and coconut milk. Cook over medium heat, whisking constantly, 2 minutes or until mixture is thick and bubbly. Stir in curry paste and next 3 ingredients. Stir chicken, green beans, and red bell pepper strips into curry mixture; cook 2 minutes or until thoroughly heated. Stir in 2 Tbsp. chopped cilantro. Serve chicken mixture over rice. Sprinkle with remaining chopped cilantro. Serve with lime wedges.

Simple Swap

If you're a fan of the super-spicy, try adding an extra tablespoon of curry paste. If not, scale back to 2 table-spoons for less spice but noticeable flavor.

Grab and Go!

For an easy side dish to tame the spice, serve with fresh mangoes or oranges.

❑ *mangoes*

❑ *oranges*

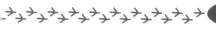
Chicken-and-Sausage Jambalaya

Makes 6 servings **Hands-on Time:** 14 min. **Total Time:** 44 min.

1 lb. smoked sausage, cut into ¼-inch-thick slices
1 medium-size green bell pepper, chopped
1 small onion, chopped
2 (10-oz.) cans mild diced tomatoes and green chiles
1 (14-oz.) can chicken broth

1 tsp. garlic powder
1 tsp. Cajun seasoning
3 cups chopped rotisserie chicken
2 cups uncooked long-grain rice
Garnish: 2 Tbsp. sliced green onions

1. Cook sausage in a Dutch oven over medium heat, stirring occasionally, 5 minutes.

2. Add bell pepper and onion; cook, stirring occasionally, 3 minutes or until vegetables are tender.

3. Stir in tomatoes and green chiles, broth, 1 cup water, garlic powder, and Cajun seasoning; bring to a boil, stirring occasionally. Stir in chicken and rice. Cover, reduce heat, and simmer 30 minutes or until rice is tender. Sprinkle with green onions, if desired.

FROM THE KITCHEN

This recipe tastes just as delicious the next day. Store leftovers in an airtight container for up to two days.

Simple Swap

For an extra kick of flavor, add an additional teaspoon of Cajun seasoning to the mix.

This elegant dinner will wow family and friends, and it won't take more than 30 minutes to prep.

Simple Swap

For a twist on these tasty shells, use ricotta cheese in place of cottage cheese.

Pronto-Stuffed Pasta Shells

Makes 4 to 6 servings **Hands-on Time:** 30 min.
Total Time: 1 hr., 20 min.

18 jumbo pasta shells
2 (10-oz.) packages frozen chopped spinach, thawed
2 cups chopped rotisserie chicken
1 (16-oz.) container 1% low-fat cottage cheese

1 large egg, lightly beaten
¼ cup grated Parmesan cheese
1 Tbsp. chopped fresh basil
¼ tsp. ground nutmeg
1 (16-oz.) jar Alfredo sauce

1. Preheat oven to 350°. Prepare pasta shells according to package directions.
2. Meanwhile, drain chopped spinach well, pressing between paper towels.
3. Stir together spinach, chicken, and next 5 ingredients. Spoon mixture evenly into shells.
4. Spread half of jarred Alfredo sauce in a lightly greased 13- x 9-inch baking dish. Arrange stuffed pasta shells over sauce, and pour remaining sauce over shells.
5. Bake, covered, at 350° for 40 to 45 minutes or until filling is hot and sauce is bubbly. Remove from oven, and let stand 10 minutes.

FROM THE KITCHEN

To make ahead, prepare recipe as directed through Step 4. Cover and freeze for up to 1 month. Thaw in refrigerator 24 hours. Let stand at room temperature 30 minutes. Bake, covered, for 1 hour and 20 minutes.

One-Dish Chicken Pasta

Makes 6 servings **Hands-on Time:** 30 min. **Total Time:** 30 min.

1 (12-oz.) package farfalle (bow-tie) pasta
5 Tbsp. butter, divided
1 medium onion, chopped
1 medium-size red bell pepper, chopped
1 (8-oz.) package fresh mushrooms, quartered
⅓ cup all-purpose flour
3 cups chicken broth
2 cups milk
3 cups chopped rotisserie chicken
1 cup (4 oz.) shredded Parmesan cheese
1 tsp. pepper
½ tsp. salt
Toppings: toasted sliced almonds, chopped fresh flat-leaf parsley, shredded Parmesan cheese

1. Prepare pasta according to package directions. Meanwhile, melt 2 Tbsp. butter in a Dutch oven over medium heat. Add onion and bell pepper; sauté 5 minutes or until tender. Add mushrooms; sauté 4 minutes. Remove from Dutch oven.
2. Melt remaining 3 Tbsp. butter in Dutch oven over low heat; whisk in flour until smooth. Cook, whisking constantly, 1 minute. Gradually whisk in chicken broth and milk; cook over medium heat, whisking constantly, 5 to 7 minutes or until thickened and bubbly.
3. Stir chicken, sautéed vegetables, and hot cooked pasta into sauce. Add cheese, pepper, and salt. Serve with desired toppings.

Toasted almonds are a terrific topping, but they can also be mixed into the dish after the cheese is added.

FROM THE KITCHEN

To toast almonds, preheat oven to 350°, and bake almonds for 4 to 6 minutes or until toasted and fragrant.

Chicken Spaghetti

Makes 6 to 8 servings **Hands-on Time:** 15 min. **Total Time:** 25 min.

1 (12-oz.) package spaghetti
1 medium onion, chopped
1 small green bell pepper, chopped
Vegetable cooking spray
1 (14½-oz.) can Italian-style stewed tomatoes
1 (14-oz.) can chicken broth
1 (6-oz.) can Italian-style tomato paste
1 (16-oz.) package pasteur-ized prepared cheese product, cubed
3 cups chopped rotisserie chicken

1. Prepare spaghetti according to package directions. Drain and keep warm.

2. Meanwhile, sauté onion and bell pepper in a Dutch oven coated with cooking spray over medium-high heat 3 to 4 minutes. Stir in tomatoes, broth, and tomato paste.

3. Bring to a boil; reduce heat, and simmer 10 minutes. Stir in cheese; cook 1 minute or until cheese melts. Stir in pasta and chicken; cook 2 to 3 minutes or until thoroughly heated.

Grab and Go!

Some toasted garlic bread is all you need to serve alongside this creamy spaghetti.

❏ *1 loaf garlic bread, toasted*

Metric Equivalents

The information in the following charts is provided to help cooks outside the United States successfully use the recipes in this book. All equivalents are approximate.

EQUIVALENTS FOR DIFFERENT TYPES OF INGREDIENTS

Standard Cup	Fine Powder (ex. flour)	Grain (ex. rice)	Granular (ex. sugar)	Liquid Solids (ex. butter)	Liquid (ex. milk)
1	140 g	150 g	190 g	200 g	240 ml
¾	105 g	113 g	143 g	150 g	180 ml
⅔	93 g	100 g	125 g	133 g	160 ml
½	70 g	75 g	95 g	100 g	120 ml
⅓	47 g	50 g	63 g	67 g	80 ml
¼	35 g	38 g	48 g	50 g	60 ml
⅛	18 g	19 g	24 g	25 g	30 ml

DRY INGREDIENTS BY WEIGHT

(To convert ounces to grams, multiply the number of ounces by 30.)

1 oz	= ¹⁄₁₆ lb	=	30 g
4 oz	= ¼ lb	=	120 g
8 oz	= ½ lb	=	240 g
12 oz	= ¾ lb	=	360 g
16 oz	= 1 lb	=	480 g

LENGTH

(To convert inches to centimeters, multiply the number of inches by 2.5.)

1 in	=		2.5 cm
6 in	= ½ ft	=	15 cm
12 in	= 1 ft	=	30 cm
36 in	= 3 ft	= 1 yd	= 90 cm
40 in	=		100 cm = 1 m

LIQUID INGREDIENTS BY VOLUME

¼ tsp =			1 ml
½ tsp =			2 ml
1 tsp =			5 ml
3 tsp = 1 Tbsp =		½ fl oz =	15 ml
2 Tbsp =	⅛ cup =	1 fl oz =	30 ml
4 Tbsp =	¼ cup =	2 fl oz =	60 ml
5⅓ Tbsp =	⅓ cup =	3 fl oz =	80 ml
8 Tbsp =	½ cup =	4 fl oz =	120 ml
10⅔ Tbsp =	⅔ cup =	5 fl oz =	160 ml
12 Tbsp =	¾ cup =	6 fl oz =	180 ml
16 Tbsp =	1 cup =	8 fl oz =	240 ml
1 pt =	2 cups =	16 fl oz =	480 ml
1 qt =	4 cups =	32 fl oz =	960 ml
		33 fl oz =	1000 ml = 1 l

COOKING/OVEN TEMPERATURES

	Fahrenheit	Celsius	Gas Mark
Freeze Water	32° F	0° C	
Room Temperature	68° F	20° C	
Boil Water	212° F	100° C	
Bake	325° F	160° C	3
	350° F	180° C	4
	375° F	190° C	5
	400° F	200° C	6
	425° F	220° C	7
	450° F	230° C	8
Broil			Grill

Index

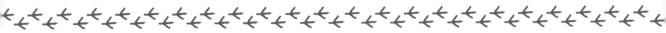

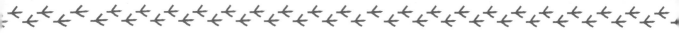

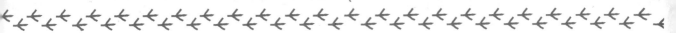

ISBN-13: 978-0-8487-3702-3
ISBN-10: 0-8487-3702-4

ISBN-13: 978-0-8487-3827-3
ISBN-10: 0-8487-3827-6

ISBN-13: 978-0-8487-3987-4
ISBN-10: 0-8487-3987-6

ISBN-13: 978-0-8487-3988-1
ISBN-10: 0-8487-3988-4

Library of Congress Control Number: 2012940621

Printed in the United States of America
First Printing 2012

Oxmoor House

Editorial Director: Leah McLaughlin
Creative Director: Felicity Keane
Senior Brand Manager: Daniel Fagan
Senior Editor: Rebecca Brennan
Managing Editor: Rebecca Benton

Southern Living® Rotisserie Chicken Cookbook

Editor: Allison Cox
Project Editor: Megan McSwain Yeatts
Assistant Designer: Allison Sperando Potter
Director, Test Kitchen: Elizabeth Tyler Austin
Assistant Directors, Test Kitchen: Julie Christopher, Julie Gunter
Recipe Developers and Testers: Wendy Ball, R.D.; Victoria E. Cox; Stefanie Maloney; Callie Nash; Leah Van Deren
Recipe Editor: Alyson Moreland Haynes
Food Stylists: Margaret Monroe Dickey, Catherine Crowell Steele
Photography Director: Jim Bathie
Senior Photo Stylist: Kay E. Clarke
Photo Stylist: Katherine Eckert Coyne
Assistant Photo Stylist: Mary Louise Menendez
Production Manager: Theresa Beste-Farley

Contributors

Project Editor: Laura Hoxworth
Copy Editor: Rhonda Lother
Proofreaders: Norma Butterworth-McKittrick, Dolores Hydock
Recipe Developers and Testers: Tamara Goldis, Erica Hopper, Tonya Johnson, Kyra Moncrief, Kathleen Royal Phillips
Indexer: Mary Ann Laurens
Interns: Erin Bishop; Morgan Bolling; Mackenzie Cogle; Jessica Cox, R.D.; Alicia Lavender; Anna Pollock; Ashley White
Photographers: Beau Gustafson, Mary Britton Senseney
Photo Stylists: Mary Clayton Carl, Caitlin Van Horn

Southern Living®

Editor: M. Lindsay Bierman
Creative Director: Robert Perino
Managing Editor: Candace Higginbotham
Art Director: Chris Hoke
Executive Editors: Rachel Hardage Barrett, Jessica S. Thuston
Food Director: Shannon Sliter Satterwhite
Test Kitchen Director: Rebecca Kracke Gordon
Senior Writer: Donna Florio
Senior Food Editor: Mary Allen Perry
Recipe Editor: JoAnn Weatherly
Assistant Recipe Editor: Ashley Arthur
Test Kitchen Specialist/Food Styling: Vanessa McNeil Rocchio
Test Kitchen Professionals: Norman King, Pam Lolley, Angela Sellers
Senior Photographers: Ralph Lee Anderson, Gary Clark, Art Meripol
Photographers: Robbie Caponetto, Laurey W. Glenn
Photo Research Coordinator: Ginny P. Allen
Senior Photo Stylist: Buffy Hargett
Editorial Assistant: Pat York

Time Home Entertainment Inc.

Publisher: Jim Childs
VP, Strategy & Business Development: Steven Sandonato
Executive Director, Marketing Services: Carol Pittard
Executive Director, Retail & Special Sales: Tom Mifsud
Executive Director, New Product Development: Peter Harper
Director, Bookazine Development & Marketing: Laura Adam
Publishing Director: Joy Butts
Finance Director: Glenn Buonocore
Assistant General Counsel: Helen Wan

To order additional publications,
call 1-800-765-6400 or 1-800-491-0551.

For more books to enrich your life, visit oxmoorhouse.com

To search, savor, and share thousands
of recipes, visit myrecipes.com

Cover: Buffalo Chicken Pizza (page 29); Double-Crust Chicken Pot Pie (page 45)

Back Cover: Chicken Corncakes (page 51); Easy Chicken and Dumplings (page 59); Southwest Chicken Mac and Cheese (page 15); Chicken, Apple, and Smoked Gouda Salad (page 84); Chicken Stir-Fry (page 111); Chicken-and-Broccoli Salad (page 179); One-Dish Chicken Pasta (page 217)